John
Kenneth
Galbraith
and the
Lower
Economics

John
Kenneth
Galbraith
and the
Lower
Economics

Myron E. Sharpe

SECOND EDITION

International Arts and Sciences Press, Inc. **iasp** White Plains, N.Y.

In honor of my mother;
in memory of my father

Contents

Preface

to the Second Edition

The provocation for a second edition of this book is the appearance of *Economics and the Public Purpose,* Galbraith's culminating work in the series examined within. His new effort had to be reckoned with. Yet I was reluctant to tamper with what had already been written. A completed book has an independent existence and is no longer part of the author. The addition of a new chapter seemed like an intrusion comparable to grafting a third arm onto a statue. Fortunately a review editorial and an interview with Galbraith were available. Both appeared in *Challenge: The Magazine of Economic Affairs* at the time that *Economics and the Public Purpose* was issued in 1973. They cover all the important points that I would wish to discuss. These items have been introduced as a postscript.

Possessed of present knowledge, I would alter only one thing in the first edition, and that is my conclusion. It would now have to be more favorable to Galbraith. In the spacious context of *Economics and the Public Purpose,* which deals with the total economy, disagreements about profit maximization, consumer sovereignty and the technostructure become less significant and Galbraith's realism about the essential character of the economy rises into proper perspective. Concentrated power and uneven development *are* the salient facts of modern economics. They are *not* the main preoccupation of traditional economics. Galbraith's obsessive drumming on these facts is what makes him appear so wrongheaded to those who are bewitched by laissez-faire assumptions and so liberated to those who are not.

Today the cry is heard: "Where is the new Keynes?" The majority of economists, the monetary-fiscalists, are in disarray; they know how to handle inflation and recession separately but not simultaneously. If they intend to wait for a new Keynes who will think up a clever device to alleviate stagflation while leaving all social, political and economic relations intact, they are likely to have an extremely long wait. That leaves the monetarists, who would cure inflation with a resounding recession; and the planners, headed by Galbraith, whose program and strategy are set out in all necessary detail in the last third of *Economics and the Public Purpose.* Considering the prospects of the first two groups, both free market loyalists to the end, it is just possible that the day will arrive in the not too distant future when the President will say: "We are all Galbraithians now."

MES

White Plains, New York
September 1974

Preface
to the First Edition

In *Ambassador's Journal*, John Kenneth Galbraith acknowledged that he was "without rival as the nation's first expert on the price of hogs." The present book will not deal with hog prices. Price theory belongs to the higher learning, and this essay does not venture into that realm. But the very mention of hog prices does bring to mind the fact that Galbraith is a man of many callings. The *Journal* was written while he was Ambassador to India under John F. Kennedy—or was it under Dean Rusk? Since then he has been Chairman of the ADA, President of the American Economic Association, advisor to would-be presidents and general public irritant. During World War II Galbraith was chief price-fixer in the OPA and from that experience came his most scholarly book, *A Theory of Price Control*. In Galbraith's opinion it is his best book. I am inclined to agree. It is also his most unread book and comes in a plain brown wrapper instead of a colorful dust jacket. The resulting trauma led Galbraith to resolve never to write a book for economists again. He has never deviated from that resolution.

The essay in your hands has nothing to do with any of these things. Rather it is about only one aspect of Galbraith's activities and thought, but that aspect happens to be the most important: his writings in political economics. The high theme of these writings is that we live in an economy of concentrated economic power. Textbook theory fails to explain this economy; it deals with bygone days. Galbraith's job is to push, drag, cajole and finesse economics into the latter half of the twentieth century. An important part of that job is to convince the public that the commonly accepted goals of economic growth and full employment—variously defined by Republicans and Democrats—are obsolete. The purpose of the economy should not be simply to produce more of anything that happens to get produced. "The question now is *what* we produce and *for whom* and *on what* terms." That chord was first sounded in *The Affluent Society,* an ironic title which describes a society that has the wealth to solve its problems if only it has the will.

Power and politics have been removed from economics and must be put back if economics is to regain its connection with reality. The most cherished tenet in the history of economic thought is that of the marvelous self-regulatory free market. Admit that the market is self-regulating, and the issue of power disappears from economics. Deny it, and power reappears. The steady preoccupation of the mature Galbraith is to deny it; to assert that the modern economy is incapable of self-regulation; and to deny that it can be made capable of it.

The antitrust faction has spent a century arguing the opposite case. Bust the trusts. Power will be removed from the marketplace and self-regulating free competition will be restored. Impossible, says Galbraith. Bigness is a *fait accompli*. You can nibble here and nibble there with antitrust suits, but unless you are willing to dismantle two-thirds of the economy, you can't go back to the textbook market. The antitrusters have, like Don Quixote battling the windmill, tried with might and main to do it. But *really* to do it means all-out war against big business. The revolutionary implications are just too staggering for a man of Galbraith's moderate disposition to contemplate.

The alternative to antitrust is to accept bigness and to regulate it. That requires not just a regulatory device but a political movement that can win over public opinion. Winning over public opinion is the first step in emancipating the state from corporate power. The reader will find the clearest statement of Galbraith's program in *Who Needs the Democrats* and of his principles in the 1972 Presidential Address to the American Economic Association. No doubt the Democrats will try many of the things to be found in these documents when they get the chance.

Galbraith's views have manifestly evolved over the years. The ideas which were frozen into print in 1952 or 1958 are not all necessarily the ideas of the present Galbraith. Criticism of them is therefore not necessarily criticism of the present Galbraith. But if the reader approaches Galbraith (and this essay) with Galbraith's underlying assumptions firmly in mind, then various details of analysis with which the reader—as well as Galbraith—may or may not agree, will appear secondary, and the larger picture will emerge.

Only one question remains, and that is, why I wrote this book. A preface is the place for confessions, and so it is not wrong to admit that I wrote this book because I admire Galbraith. To identify important problems requires a special gift; Galbraith has it. But admiration does not require agreement, and since one confession leads to another, I must further admit that the book turned out to be far more critical than I had anticipated. To start with approbation and end with faultfinding is, I suppose, one of the hazards of writing anything longer than a one-page letter. While it would not be quite accurate to say that I agree with Galbraith about everything in general and nothing in particular, some such formula will have to do until I can think of a better one. The result of this posture is a friendly polemical discussion of some disputed questions of political economy.

MES

White Plains, New York
February 1973

A Note on Sources and Page References

The editions of John Kenneth Galbraith's works used in this book are:

American Capitalism: The Concept of Countervailing Power, New and Revised Edition, 1956. The first edition was published in 1952.

The Affluent Society, Second, Revised Edition, 1971. The first edition was published in 1958.

The New Industrial State, Second Edition, Revised, 1971. The first edition was published in 1967.

Economics and the Public Purpose, 1973.

These four books were issued by Houghton Mifflin Company, Boston.

In Chapters 2, 3, and 4 of this book, page references, unless otherwise noted, refer to pages in the editions listed above.

John
Kenneth
Galbraith
and the
Lower
Economics

CHAPTER 1

A Revolution in Economics?

THE LOWER ECONOMICS referred to in the title of this book was suggested by a figure of speech once used by Galbraith. He pictured the prestige structure of economics as a hollow pyramid or cone. At the base the sides are transparent and have many openings to the outside. As one approaches the apex, the sides become increasingly opaque and impermeable. Economists dealing with practical matters dwell at the base, and they have easy communication with the outside world. Their economics is adulterated by foreign admixtures of politics, moral judgments and sociology. The practitioner at this level merits little esteem. In contrast, economists dealing with pure theory can be found near the top of the pyramid. They are protected from outside influence. Their work is formal and mathematical. It has little or nothing to do with reality, and is very highly regarded by the profession.

Galbraith's mockery makes it perfectly clear where he thinks the valuable work in economics is being done. He himself occupies a position near the base of the pyramid and practices the lower economics, which, far from being a term of opprobrium, must in this view be considered an accolade. The abstractness so much admired by contemporary economists is not suited to the work which Galbraith sets for himself. He is not, in Robert Solow's phrase describing economists, a "determined little thinker," but a determined big thinker.[1] He is not interested in refining a small part of the doctrine, but in recasting and reassembling the whole. The compelling reason for this is that the economy has changed while theory has stood still. The starting point of neoclassical economics is the small firm, the market and consumer sovereignty, as the reader can readily verify by consulting Paul A. Samuelson's ubiquitous *Economics*. Galbraith's starting point is the large firm, planning and producer sovereignty. Neoclassical economics takes it for granted that the growth of production is a good thing. Galbraith does not, for the growth of GNP may be accompanied by a decline in the quality of life.

Galbraith's efforts are nothing short of an attempted revolution in economic science. The test of this assertion is not his personality, style or program, but—obviously —his economics. Galbraith does not *appear* to be a revolutionary because in person he is urbane, in style elegant and in program well within the compass of reform. We must not be put off by such considerations. Keynes had the same characteristics. But he led a revolution in economics by attacking and destroying crucial assumptions of the discipline. If the assumptions adverted to in the previous paragraph—relating to consumer and firm behavior and the honorable status of production *per se*—

1. Economists are so defined in a sparkling exchange with Galbraith. *The Public Interest,* Fall 1967.

are successfully challenged, then the Galbraithian revolution will be far more sweeping than the Keynesian. Keynes convinced his colleagues that underemployment equilibrium was possible in the absence of sufficient effective demand and that, in order to put things to rights, a government must spend (or induce spending) rather than retrench. As a result, macrotheory, which had been part of the underworld of Major Douglas and other cranks, was accorded a high place alongside microtheory. But microtheory was left untouched. The Galbraithian attack is two-pronged: one against each branch of theory. If it were to succeed, the whole of neoclassical economics would come crashing down.

Several requirements must be met for a revolution in a science to be successful.[2] The science must encounter difficulties in explaining facts; an alternative, consistently logical framework of explanation must be made available; and a conversion must take place among communicants of the field of study. There is no need for the reader to wait in suspense before discovering the author's views. The first point will be conceded; the latter two denied. Neoclassical economics began with laissez-faire assumptions and by accretions and qualifications has attempted to remain relevant to industrial society. We shall agree with Galbraith that modern economics suffers from striking anomalies and is ready for renovation. We are

2. Thomas S. Kuhn is the first (to my knowledge) to discuss revolutions in science methodically. See *The Structure of Scientific Revolutions,* The University of Chicago Press, 1962. A second edition with a reply to critics was published in 1970. Benjamin Ward took up the idea of scientific revolutions and applied it to contemporary economics in *What's Wrong with Economics?* Basic Books, 1972.

unable to concede that he has effected an entirely successful revolution in theory. And it goes without saying that no conversion of the profession has taken place.

Galbraith is often criticized for painting on too broad a canvas, for not being a "little thinker." The big thinker allegedly cannot assimilate all the details of the subdisciplines of economics and must inevitably make a mess of things. Solow puts it this way: it is better to investigate the effect on auto and housing production of a ten percent surcharge on personal and corporate income than to study "Whither We Are Trending." To the contrary. Everyone, undoubtedly including Professor Solow, wants to know whither we're trending as much as, if not more than, he wants to know about the effects of a tax surcharge. The juxtaposition of these two types of questions could be put down as a debating device were there not a deeper issue embedded in this bit of raillery. The methodology of formalist economics dictates that the only questions to be entertained are those which can be asked and answered with precision, preferably by means of econometrics, statistics or game theory. Awkward questions that do not fit in must be abandoned to sociology. The result is that more and more can be said about less and less, and we find ourselves rising in Galbraith's pyramid to levels where the walls become impenetrable and the occupants subsist on pure thoughts.

Galbraith has been called by some an institutional economist, and I think there is merit in so classifying him. The institutionalists are a very loose American grouping originating with Thorstein Veblen, and what they have in common is the view that the economy ought to be studied as a part of human culture. Veblen thought that the model should be not physics, but cultural anthropology. Economists should concern themselves with the actual institutions of society rather than try to make generalizations about abstract relationships that have no reference to time or place. Although the institutionalists are in the minority, and thought to be slightly disreputable, we shall nevertheless take the view that economics will not be harmed by occasional infusions of reality.

The lower economics is institutional economics, and it possesses its own method, which has been aptly called storytelling.[3] Storytelling is the device required by the person who wants to make a rational statement about a subject like anthropology, history or economics in its actual institutional setting. The storyteller must knit together all the relevant facts, theories and values required to tell a coherent and convincing story. The facts must be verifiable, the theories germane and the values compelling.[4] Those who are dismayed that storytelling is cruder than mathematical model building may be consoled by the fact that the subject matter itself is crude and does not always lend itself to elegant treatment. Above all, value, fact and theory cannot be tightly locked into separate compartments. What is GNP? It is usually treated as fact (data), but it also intermingles theory (this is the correct thing to measure) and value (the bigger the better). At first GNP looks quite objective and value-free, but *ought* keeps sneaking back in where it was thought to have been banished, and while we start with what seems a mere measure of economic

---

3. A disquisition on storytelling can be found in *What's Wrong with Economics?* pp. 179-190; but to understand these pages it is necessary to read the whole book.

4. Some rules for verifying a story are offered by Ward on p. 189 of his book.

activity, we end with a somewhat fuzzy measure of good (more of it) and bad (less of it). Social science tries hard to avoid saying what people *ought* to want but says it anyway. Market theory assumes that consumers want what they want because they want it. But with this assumption comes the implicit judgment that in a market economy the existing pattern of distribution of goods and services (whatever it is) is best, and that it is no business of the economist to second-guess people about their preferences.

The practitioner of the lower economics does not so deceive himself. He prefers to make explicit the interplay of value between the observer and the observed. The fear that Galbraith is substituting the judgment of the observer for that of the observed strikes terror in the hearts of economists. But that is because of a misapprehension. He is simply explicit about his values while others are so much in the habit of being implicit that they have come to think that as scientists they haven't any values at all (other than truth seeking and that sort of thing). One could say with some precision that value is to the economist as sex is to the Victorian: it must be hushed up. But we all know about the astonishing manifestations of sex when it is hushed up. Unfortunately economics is a repressed science and Galbraith has tried to help overcome its inhibitions. Regrettably the analysis is still at the stage where the analyst is resented.

If Galbraith's willingness to discuss broad issues succeeds in influencing others to do likewise, he will have made no small contribution to economics, quite apart from the substantive aspect of his efforts. Far from being *avant-garde,* a move in the direction of accepting broad inquiry as a legitimate function of economics would in a

sense be a *counter*revolution, since i
great tradition of the doyens of ecoi
Smith to Maynard Keynes, who did ir.
fear of Thinking Big. With this subv
shall leave speculation and proceed
braith's three major books.

CHAPTER 2

American Capitalism

AMERICAN CAPITALISM IS the first of John Kenneth Galbraith's major books and the only one having about it an aura of complacency. It was published in 1952 during the postwar celebration of free enterprise and it bears the birthmarks of that euphoric epoch. Subsequently, Galbraith was to become more critical, less accepting, sterner in his judgment of the American economy. The task of *American Capitalism* was to explain why it works; the task of subsequent books was to explain why it fails. *American Capitalism* starts with the declaration that the competitive model cannot explain the *modus operandi* of modern industrialism. Events have passed it by; it is no longer relevant. Before his later disenchantment, Galbraith sought another automatic mechanism within the very structure of capitalism which would make clear why it continued to operate rather than fall apart. This mechanism he found in the theory of countervailing power, the central subject of his book. He subsequently abandoned the theory. It does not appear again in his works. Yet it is a line of thinking still worth examining.

The collapse of the competitive model

Frequently in his writings Galbraith stops to cast an admiring glance at the competitive model, the theory of a free enterprise economy so assiduously constructed by generations of economists. The days when this model seemed to reflect reality are not sufficiently distant for its hypnotic effects to fail to influence them. The competitive model solved so many problems so brilliantly. But this elegant structure received a smashing blow in the Great Depression. The exception became the rule. Concentration in industry was matched by a counter-concentration of labor in trade unions. Entry into many industries was barred by prohibitive capital requirements. Say's Law of Markets was laid to rest when it became apparent that buying and selling were two separate acts and that a person did not have to buy after he had sold. Prices and the volume of goods produced were no longer determined automatically in the concentrated sector of business. Instead they were determined by the decisions of private persons in the managements of large corporations. Monopoly opened the door to prices above and quantities below the competitive level. In fact, among the giants of industry prices were outlawed as a weapon of competition and replaced by competition based on product differentiation and advertising. Uncertainty was introduced into the economic game: the observer could no longer be sure what moves the players would make under given assumptions. Of course we are speaking about a rather abstract kind of uncertainty—how the players would act according to the dictates of the model. But the players themselves felt uncertainty no less under competitive capitalism than under oligopolistic capitalism. That very uncertainty was undoubtedly one of the forces which motivated the change.

Concentration in industry and labor carried an anticoncentration movement in its wake. The antitrust point of view is often a naive nostalgia for an idyllic past when competition prevailed. Some antitrusters would restore the regime of small competitive units in order to obtain the alleged benefits: optimum prices and outputs and freedom from business fluctuations. Monopoly means privilege and antitrusters would abolish privilege.

If there is anything consistent in Galbraith's public position through the years, it is his contemptuous opposition to the cause of antitrust. "It is possible to prosecute a few evildoers; it is evidently not so practical to indict a whole economy" (p. 52). And: "To suppose that there are grounds for antitrust prosecution wherever three, four or a half dozen firms dominate a market is to suppose that the very fabric of American capitalism is illegal" (p. 55). One of the pillars of Galbraith's doctrine is that it is not only chimerical to try to return to the competitive model; it would destroy the productive achievements of American capitalism.

While the antitrust view emphasized the harmful effects of the transformation from laissez-faire to managed capitalism, another trend of thought, represented by Joseph Schumpeter and Karl Polanyi, emphasized the necessary and constructive aspects of this transition. Galbraith is an adherent of this point of view. In *Socialism, Capitalism and Democracy,* Schumpeter depicted the process of industrial concentration as one in which firms built up protective walls around themselves to shield their activities from the depredations of competitive uncertainty. Businessmen did not think as much of exposing capital investments to the risks of the open market as did economic theorists. They preferred the safety of size and the freedom size gave them to control prices, quantities and the labor market and to obtain the time required to nurture new ventures. The optima of competitive prices, outputs and profits were sacrificed; but that sacrifice put the concentrated industries in a position to protect their investments, cultivate innovations behind shielding walls and obtain the higher profits that enabled them to do so. The net result was a more productive economic machine. The major compensation for efficiency, lost by giving up the competitive model, was technical change. Large firms are excellent instruments for inducing technical change and are admirably equipped for financing it. This Schumpeterian argument is essentially taken over by Galbraith who makes the ultimate retort to those who yearn for a return to the competitive model: they talk about inefficiency yet acknowledge that the modern economy is vastly more productive than its competitive predecessor.

A similar view in rather broader social terms was sketched out by Polanyi in *The Great Transformation*. The laissez-faire philosophy attempted to cut off the economy from the rest of social life and force it to operate autonomously. This effort was historically unprecedented. The economy had always been a part of the polity and had never operated independently as a piece of machinery. No sooner had free competition prevailed than each sector of the polity reacted to protect itself from the uncertainties entailed. Much business, as we have seen, became centralized and concentrated. Labor organized unions for the maintenance of wages and the improvement of working conditions. Farmers organized cooperatives and ultimately obtained the support of the government to maintain parity with other sectors of the economy. Intervention by different economic classes was in spontaneous reaction to the untenable situation produced by laissez-faire. Laissez-faire was not good for anyone; everyone sought protection from it.

The uniqueness of Galbraith's views on monopoly and competition is to be found in his emphasis on technology. "Technical development is all but certain to be one of the instruments of commercial rivalry when the number of firms is small" (p. 89). Most economists discuss the suppression of patents; but they do not acknowledge the need to protect existing investments in plant and machinery. They carefully scrutinize large firms which hold back innovations from public use; they say nothing of industries in which small firms and competition are typical and in which innovations do not take place at all. Galbraith's recurring theme is that the slight decline of efficiency in concentrated industries is more than offset by large gains from technical development. Contrast oil, a concentrated and technically progressive industry, with bituminous coal, a dispersed and stagnant one. "Thus, while the incentives in the American economy do not, at any given moment, act to encourage the largest possible production at the lowest possible price, this is not the tragedy that it appears to be at first glance" (pp. 93-94).[1]

_1_. Galbraith has been taken to task for his assertions about the petroleum industry by John Jewkes, David Sawers and Richard Stillerman in _The Sources of Invention,_ W. W. Norton, 1958 and 1969. These gentlemen aver that most of the radical departures came from outside the industry or from smaller firms. See pp. 133 and 207. The retort, I suppose, is

Galbraith goes even further, arguing that "the competition of the competitive model . . . almost completely precludes technical development" (p. 86). But this is surely misstating the case. The industrial revolution and the advent of competitive capitalism are coterminous. The industrial revolution is marked by a rapid increase in productivity: that is its hallmark as nothing else is. Once industrial invention got going, it was self-sustaining. Competition forced each entrepreneur to keep costs to a minimum. The most dramatic way of reducing costs was to introduce cost-saving methods and equipment. True, these inventions were made by scattered individuals in small toolsheds and barns and cannot be compared with the organized research that is conducted by regiments of technicians today. Yet Galbraith is quite wrong in ruling out technical development in the very era in which it got its start.

Further, Galbraith errs in arguing that only large firms today can afford to support research and development. It is true in some cases, such as space, that only the largest firms, handsomely subsidized by the government, can handle the required R&D. But most of the new products introduced in the postwar period originated from individual inventions or from research conducted by small and medium-sized firms. Let it suffice to cite a representative list of better known items: "electric ranges, electric refrigerators, electric dryers, electric dishwashers, the hermetically sealed compressor used in refrigerators and air conditioners, vacuum cleaners, clothes washing machines,

that the leaders of the petroleum industry had not only the brains to use the new processes but also the sizable means required to develop them.

13

deep freezers, and electric irons, including the steam variety."[2]

The difficulty is that Galbraith doesn't distinguish between the sources of invention and their application. Many inventions originated with individuals or small firms but could be produced and marketed successfully only by giant corporations because of capital and time requirements. Most large corporations are sufficiently diversified to afford the risk of introducing major new products. Typically a small firm pioneers development and production, and after the product has proven its value, a large firm takes over, buying out or squeezing out the small one. Yet this line of development is far from universal: witness the many small, high-technology firms around Cambridge, Princeton and Stanford which have been built on patents in electronics and communications.

It simply cannot be proved that oligopoly is a superior institution for raising productivity. True, the average rate of annual productivity increase in the quarter century before World War I was 2.2 percent whereas it has been over 3 percent since World War II. But the largest sectoral rise in the recent period was in agriculture, which is not known for a high degree of concentration. We have already noted that most inventions—paramount in productivity increases—originated outside concentrated industry. Nevertheless we lack definite knowledge as to

2. *America, Inc.*, by Morton Mintz and Jerry S. Cohen, The Dial Press, 1971. Quote on p. 44. The pioneering work is *The Sources of Invention*, referred to in the previous footnote. More than half of 70 major inventions of the twentieth century originated with independent inventors.

what kinds of institutions are most conducive to scientific and technological progress. The problem is complicated by the fact that science itself is an institution with its own internal logic of development. Since the scientific enterprise has fared best in nations having institutional diversity we cannot in justice award laurels to oligopoly alone. All we can safely acknowledge is that enterprise stability due to size is very likely one among several reasons for the growth of productivity.

The theory of countervailing power

Having made a case for the productive virtues of the large modern corporation operating in the context of stimulative fiscal policy administered by a benign central government, Galbraith proceeds to wonder why any good comes of it, so far as the public is concerned, in the absence of government regulation or planning. Just at a time when no one could claim that the invisible hand was pulling the economic levers which rationalized production and distribution, things appeared to be going extremely well. The accepted explanatory principle no longer applied; no new one was at hand; Galbraith attempted to supply it. In place of the invisible hand of Adam Smith, he conjured up a new one. It is not true that all effective restraint on private power has disappeared, he advised. A counterpart of competition exists in countervailing power. Private economic power is held in check by the countervailing power of those who are subject to it. The first begets the second.

Unlike competition, which provides active restraint from the same side of the market, countervailing power provides restraint from the other side of the market. In the typical modern market of few sellers, organized labor forms a counterweight on the other side of the market. The strongest unions are usually found in markets with the strongest corporations. Similarly, in several countries consumer cooperatives developed as a countervailing force. In the United States, retail chains perform a like function. These include food, variety and department store chains and mail order houses. To obtain the largest possible volume of sales, these retail organizations must keep the cost of goods as low as they can. Being large buyers, they are in a position to command the best discounts from producers. These benefits are passed on to the consumer.

Some industries do not enjoy the blessings of countervailing power. Residential building, for example. The typical builder is a small and powerless figure, buying material in small quantities at high cost from suppliers with effective market power—one reason for the high cost of residential housing.

Galbraith contended that "the support of countervailing power has become in modern times perhaps the major domestic peacetime function of the federal government" (p. 136). In the 1930s, labor obtained legislation supporting unions and minimum wages. Farmers obtained federal price supports. Small business obtained the blessings of fair trade laws. The federal government lent its power to redress balances that had become badly unbalanced in the move away from competition and tacitly accepted the distinction between original market power and countervailing power. By extension, the same redress can be offered to others—hired farm labor, unorganized urban workers, teachers, clerical workers, municipal employees and civil servants. Indeed, in some cases it has.

In the discussion, Galbraith enters one very important caveat. Countervailing power does not function as a restraint on market power if there is inflation. "When demand is weak the bargaining position of the strongest union deteriorates to some extent" (p. 130). However, with excess demand, there is a shift of bargaining power to sellers. Then the union and employer find it mutually advantageous to effect a coalition and pass on the cost of wage increases to consumers in the form of higher prices. The self-regulating mechanism of countervailing power is no longer effective. The wage-price spiral takes over and serves only the self-interest of the large corporation and union. "Some slack in the economy is what keeps countervailing power from being converted into a coalition against the public" (p. 196). Galbraith drew what seemed at the time to be the logical conclusion: a certain amount of unemployment and idle capacity was necessary in order to enjoy the benefits of countervailing power. The ill effects of such slack could be offset by generous social security and welfare measures. We are duty-bound to add that Galbraith subsequently abandoned this view and became a champion of full employment with wage and price controls.

Even though the theory of countervailing power is not mentioned in Galbraith's later works, it still possesses some historical substance. Various social groups have in fact converted weak positions into strong ones through organization, tacitly or overtly supported by government. It is also true that economic and political organization continues to be a way for the abused and the rejected to obtain redress. The black movement and the welfare rights movement illustrate the process. The pressure group is a well-known element in American politics. Some modest claims can therefore be made for a theory of countervailing power, but in *American Capitalism* Galbraith's claims were extravagant.[3] To complicate matters there was a vexing ambiguity in his handling of the term which made it impossible to understand exactly what he was talking about.

Is countervailing power used in the interest of the group that has the power or is it used in the interest of society as a whole? Galbraith would seem to have it both ways. It is obvious that workers gain when a union obtains higher wages but it is not so obvious how the public gains. Likewise with farmers and agricultural prices. Consumers may get some price benefits from the large-scale buying of retail chains but this has not protected them from mislabeling, false claims in advertising and harmful products. Moreover, in a discussion of *American Capitalism* at the Convention of the American Economic Association in 1954, George J. Stigler, an economist who never fails to overlook any of Galbraith's shortcomings, pointed out that only a small part of the lower retail prices of grocery and drug chains was due to lower buying prices. Much of the saving was accounted for by innovations in merchandising techniques and simplification

---

3. Subsequently Galbraith acknowledged to critics that his model was only a partial one from which more limited results could be expected. He also acknowledged that the implied criterion of the model was not the improvement of consumer welfare but the reduction of social tension. We may get higher priced coal in exchange for peace in the coal fields, for example. Hence, in the end, countervailing power was not a theoretical alternative to competition, though that seemed to be the message of the book.

of selling services. At the same meeting, Galbraith was gracious enough to admit that large retailers pass on some of the gains to consumers precisely because of—competition.

American Capitalism leaves the reader in doubt about what countervailing power countervails and what it does not countervail. The theory fits into Polanyi's more general framework explaining the response of different classes to laissez-faire capitalism. Countervailing power is in part a substitute for the regulatory mechanism of the competitive market. But it does not do all the things a competitive market is supposed to do, much less things it is not supposed to do. It does not allocate resources properly; it does not regulate prices optimally; it does not result in efficient production; it does not eliminate poverty; it does not lead to the provision of amenities and public services; nor divide life intelligently between work and leisure. What it does in an economic sense is ensure that the countervailing group has a larger share of income than it would have otherwise. In a political sense, it enhances a system of multiple centers of power, supporting what Alexis de Tocqueville called secondary institutions which stand between the individual and the government or, in the case of modern capitalism, between the individual and the large corporation. But countervailing power does not in any sense ensure equality of the contending parties which continue to function within a class structure predetermined by the development of the capitalist industrial system.

In the milieu of the 1950s, it appeared that the successes rather than the shortcomings of American capitalism were what needed explaining. Galbraith concludes on the note that "The phenomenon of countervailing power does provide a negative justification for leaving authority over production decisions in private hands" (p. 167). Later, in *The New Industrial State,* Galbraith offers the riper belief that the large corporation ought to be subject to firmer public policy constraints. But, for the present, his emphasis is on countervailing power as a practical alternative to the centralization and possible abuse of economic power. Galbraith says in effect: don't knock success; let the corporations alone. Centralized decision puts a crimp in both the timing and the quality of decision-making and it is administratively possible only where production is confined to a relatively small number of standard products. Capitalism and decentralized decision-making go hand in hand.

The only acceptable form of centralized decision is embodied in the Keynesian approach to national economic management. "The essence of the Keynesian formula consists in leaving private decisions over production, including those involving prices and wages, to the men who now make them. . . . Centralized decision is brought to bear only on the climate in which those decisions are made; it insures only that the factors influencing free and intelligent decision will lead to a private action that contributes to economic stability" (p. 178). The prospects for capitalism in the last analysis are the prospects for decentralized decision. At this later date it is tempting to add: so are the prospects for socialism.

American Capitalism depicts a world in which almost everything is neatly tied down. Galbraith disposed of the problems of optimum price and volume by asserting their lesser importance as against technological development, fostered by the great corporation. He disposed of the problem of power by asserting that countervailing power develops to keep the mighty in line. Intelligently administered fiscal policy provided a suitable environment. The active dangers were inflation with its attendant risk of modifying capitalism by requiring extensive centralized decision; and poverty, still the burden of a significant minority. There are also intimations about the "unseemly economics of opulence." The economist "is exclusively preoccupied with goods *qua* goods; in his preoccupation with goods he has not paused to reflect on the relative unimportance of the goods with which he is preoccupied" (p. 102). Efficiency was not nearly so urgent as economists thought. This observation was to be put to a quite novel use in Galbraith's next book. The whole tidy world of *American Capitalism* comes apart at the seams in *The Affluent Society*.

CHAPTER 3

The
Affluent
Society

THE AFFLUENT SOCIETY is a deeply critical book and marks a sharp turn in Galbraith's attitude toward the American economy and society. By 1958, the year of publication, the first flush of postwar prosperity had worn off. The economic impetus of the Korean War had been spent and the country was experiencing the doldrums of the Eisenhower recession of 1957-58. The passage of time had shown that deep-seated problems existed which could not be solved by conventional means. *The Affluent Society* was one of the first books to come to grips with a fundamental irony of modern capitalism. An enormously productive economic plant had been built up that had raised a majority of the population out of the depths of poverty for the first time in history. Technology enabled men to produce an abundance of goods. The expansion of the gross national product had become a test of economic success; and as it rose from year to year, albeit with some pauses in times of recession, economists and much of the public thought that the ultimate solution to economic problems had been found. The majority of people did not have to worry about food, clothing and shelter but instead were concerned with cars and home appliances. America had become an affluent society, but with all the abundance there was still something gravely wrong. Goods multiplied but the quality of life diminished. Cities became less liveable; clogged roads made travel more difficult; public transportation deteriorated; education and medical services faced a crisis; welfare services became manifestly inadequate. A substantial part of the population remained poor despite the annual rise in gross national product. To this grave social imbalance, Galbraith addressed *The Affluent Society*.

The end of the economic problem?

Galbraith's analysis proceeded once more with a contrast between a competitive economy and a highly concentrated one. He again emphasized the insecurity inherent in a competitive society which no one but the economic theorist regarded with equanimity. He restated his rationale of business concentration. "The specter that has haunted the economist has been the monopoly seeking extortionate gains at the public expense. This has dominated his thoughts. The less dramatic figure, the businessman seeking protection from the vicissitudes of the competitive economy, has been much less in his mind. That is unfortunate, for the development of the modern enterprise can be understood only as a comprehensive effort to reduce risk" (p. 98).

With the high level of technology made possible by concentrated industry, Galbraith contended, the "elimination of insecurity in economic life can be a finished business." This declaration is followed by another: "the major uncertainties of economic life (subject to some caution concerning the control of depressions) have already been eliminated" (p. 107). This is undoubtedly false. A train of exceptions comes to mind: the insecurities of illness, old age and unemployment, and those inherent in small business and agriculture, not to mention insufficient income. Galbraith himself adverts to some of these as minor qualifications to his statement. They are hardly minor. Yet there is a core of truth in Galbraith's assertion. Our ability to produce an abundance of goods is unprecedented. Relative economic security is a fact for the majority except for the disasters for which there is not yet adequate insurance. The needs of the majority of the population in marketable goods have until now never been met, and it is the implication of this fact that Galbraith asks us to ponder.

Paradoxically, the earlier economists, making a virtue of necessity, assumed that economic insecurity was essential for efficiency and economic progress. Galbraith considers this perhaps the greatest miscalculation in the history of economic ideas. For experience shows that a high level of economic security is essential for maximum production. But public policy has gone so far as virtually to identify security and production. Having achieved so much by following the path of fiscal stimulus and annual output increases, it appeared to the new Keynesian economic establishment that a formula had been found for the eventual solution of all economic problems. As average income rose, sooner or later poverty itself would be totally eliminated. "The ancient preoccupations of economic life—with equality, security and productivity have now narrowed down to a preoccupation with productivity and production" (p. 115).

Production held the paramount position. In this very fact, Galbraith finds the roots of social imbalance. The virtual worship of increasing production as a universal dissolver of tensions associated with inequality; the expectation that a steady increase in the well-being of the average man will make redistribution unnecessary: these were the basic thoughts behind the drive to expand the gross national product regardless of its composition. Yet expansion of the gross national product, regardless of the kinds of goods and services which made it up, left a vast residue of unsolved problems. With this recognition comes the obsolescence of conventional Keynesian policy and the beginnings of a new policy which, for want of any commonly accepted phrase, might be called the policy of social balance.

Galbraith lays the groundwork for his analysis of social balance (or imbalance) by first discussing how the production of privately produced goods, at the expense of public services, gained primacy in both theory and practice. Characteristically, he begins with a premise of accepted economic theory. An underlying assumption of the theory of consumer demand is that the urgency of wants does not diminish appreciably as more of them are satisfied. When physical needs are satisfied, psychologically grounded ones take over. "The concept of satiation has very little standing in economics" (p. 138). A second proposition is that wants originate with the consumer; a third is that the consumer has a preference system known to himself. These propositions are barriers against criticism of what is produced and sold. The presumption is that if a commodity is produced and sold, the consumer wanted it. If he didn't want it, it wouldn't be sold. The producer would soon get the message that he was making the wrong thing. He would make haste to find out what the consumer wanted and act accordingly. The consumer is sovereign. One may not like everything the consumer consumes; but if one holds the dignity of the individual in high esteem, it follows that there is an inviolable sanctity about his choice. The existing distribution of productive efforts in society is impregnable to criticism. Or so it seemed.

But Galbraith disputed all this by challenging the assumptions of demand theory. Some things are acquired before others; and presumably the more important things come first, implying a declining urgency of need. Wants do not necessarily originate with the consumer. A vast apparatus of salesmanship and advertising attempts to tell the consumer what he wants, with no small degree of success. Nor is the consumer a computer programmed for preferences that can be brought to bear in the marketplace at an instant's notice. His somewhat vague preferences can be crystallized by the blandishments of the producer, remarkably to the advantage of the latter. If the consumer is not sovereign—and this is a heretical thought which challenges the very foundations of the central economic tradition—it follows that everything that is sold in the market is not necessarily what the consumer really wants but might well be foisted on him unawares. That being the case, the objection against examining which array of goods and services is beneficial to the consumer and which is not falls. The composition of the gross national product, made up as it is of different goods and services, is then desanctified and enters the realm of public policy and debate.

This is essentially Galbraith's brief in attacking the theory of consumer demand. Of course a person who was never caught up in this theory of consumer demand might think that Galbraith's approach involves a great deal of unnecessary strain. To someone outside the mainstream of the economics profession, the psychological assumptions about human behavior which entered economic theory in the nineteenth century seem quaintly archaic; but to those who are educated in this doctrine, the process of disenthrallment is a laborious one.[1] Galbraith acknowledges that he himself had to go through this process in writing *The Affluent Society*. Even though he has written in several places that his books are aimed over

---

1. In an effort to be objective and value-free, the radical empiricist refrained from saying anything about the importance to a given individual of one want as opposed to another. Bread may have diminishing marginal utility to a person as he eats more of it but then he may want ice cream when he has satisfied his appetite for bread. The economist, being unable to get into the consumer's brain, believed it unscientific to say that ice cream was needed less than bread. By the same reasoning, it was thought to be objectively impossible to say anything about the relative importance of one person's wants against those of another. The millionaire may crave his Rolls Royce as intensely as the humble workman craves his loaf of brown bread. Who are economists to say differently if the relative intensity of wants cannot be measured? But we know that if a person must choose between three square meals a day 365 days a year and a Rolls Royce, he will choose to eat and reconcile himself to traveling on foot. Such commonplace observations are banned by the theory of consumer behavior.

the heads of the economics profession at the general educated public, Galbraith still has the professional economist very much in mind. He writes for the layman in order not to be ignored by the economist. And for the economist who picks up his books, Galbraith has taken the precaution of speaking the economist's language even though what he says in that language may be disagreeable.

Keynes argued that there is a range of absolute needs that can be satisfied and he reached an important conclusion (and may we add that our view that the appropriate measure of needs is socially determined, not absolute, does not alter the validity of Keynes' conclusion): "Assuming no important wars and no important increase in population, the *economic problem* may be solved, or be at least within sight of solution, within a hundred years. This means that the economic problem is not—if we look into the future—*the permanent problem of the human race*" (quoted on p. 145). The significance of *The Affluent Society* is its assertion that the time of solution has arrived: we already have the capacity to produce enough of the necessities: production has already become less urgent. But theory has failed to keep up with events and goes on insisting that production is as urgent as ever. Everyone accepts unquestioningly the proposition that the first order of business is to produce more this year than was produced last year. The government and the corporations are geared to this end and public opinion endorses it. A decade and a half after the appearance of *The Affluent Society* skepticism about this goal is much more common. But in 1958, Galbraith's assertions were quite unconventional.

The economic problem can be solved through scientific technology in the sense that the economic necessities of life can be supplied to everyone in the industrialized countries: that is the novel situation with which Galbraith wrestles. It is of secondary importance whether one thinks that we have the capacity to solve the problem now or that we will have it in ten or twenty years. Galbraith's contribution does not depend on the difference of a few years more or less. His focus on the problem is what matters. If the production of goods is less urgent, then we should have the resources to eliminate poverty and improve the quality of life—that is Galbraith's point.

Yet in another sense, the economic problem is never solved if it is defined not as the abolition of physical want but as the organization of society to satisfy wants of any nature whatever. In that case there will always be a question as to which wants are to be satisfied first. Galbraith has unnecessarily complicated the issue by insisting on the lesser importance of production and efficiency. Given a choice, it is always better to produce goods and services more efficiently rather than less so.[2] The issue is not that it is less urgent to produce goods and that therefore they may be produced less efficiently, but rather in what order goods and services are to be produced with the highest practicable efficiency.

Want creation

Having established that wants are malleable, Gal-

2. Except when a deliberate choice is made to sacrifice efficiency for a non-economic objective, such as reducing the tedium of repetitive work.

braith concentrates his attention on advertising, the mechanism by which producers manipulate the preferences of consumers. "If the individual's wants are to be urgent, they must be original with himself. They cannot be urgent if they must be contrived for him. And above all, they must not be contrived by the process of production by which they are satisfied. For this means that the whole case for the urgency of production, based on the urgency of wants, falls to the ground. One cannot defend production as satisfying wants if that production creates the wants" (pp. 146-147).

In speaking of "modern want creation" Galbraith notes the direct relationship between a firm's expenditures on production and its expenditures on "synthesizing the desires" for that production. He calls the latter the dependence effect—the creation of wants through advertising and salesmanship. "If production is to increase, the wants must be effectively contrived. In the absence of the contrivance, the increase would not occur. This is not true of all goods, but that it is true of a substantial part is sufficient" (p. 153).

As is the case with many of Galbraith's vital points, his argument is overstated and its effectiveness is undermined. He puts too great a burden on the process of advertising in attempting to explain why consumers buy goods and, later in his discussion, why they prefer marketed goods to public services. It is true that people did not and could not want refrigerators, clothes washers and cars before they were invented and put on the market. It does not follow that the want for them had to be created *ab ovo* by advertising. The needs for a convenient way of handling food, an easier way of washing clothes and a speedy and versatile mode of transportation were present, lurking in the background. For people needed to eat, wash clothes and move from one place to another. Given the removal of much of the population from farms, the desire of women to be free from the household drudgery of washing clothes by hand, and the increasing sprawl of towns and suburbs, the refrigerator, washing machine and automobile seem natural and logical choices of consumers, requiring an assist from advertising only to familiarize them with the possibilities and jar them out of set patterns of habit.

The point is made very nicely by Robin Marris in *The Economic Theory of "Managerial" Capitalism*.[3] A person may have what Marris calls a latent need, but this latent need cannot be converted into a want for a specific product until he hears that there is such a product. When he comes to want a product, it is because there was a prior latent need. "The commercial process consists of sensing the existence of latent needs and exploiting them, i.e. converting them into conscious wants by marketing and advertising appropriate products" (Marris, p. 139).

We must add that the very development of social organization itself is a cause of new wants. The growth in demand for automobiles, for example, is intimately connected with the growth of suburbia. The automobile made the suburbs possible and the suburbs made the automobile necessary. The want to use the telephone or the postal service is not original with the individual, though the want to communicate may be. The want for the telephone and postal service exists because of the social organization into which the individual was born, civilized life as we know it being impossible without them.

3. The Free Press, 1964; Basic Books, 1968.

In overstating his case, Galbraith fails to acknowledge that the producer first goes out to discover latent needs before he dreams of producing a new product. This is called market research and is an integral part of advertising and salesmanship. Its existence is an acknowledgment that the consumer cannot be maneuvered into wanting the producer's product if no latent need exists. With heavy advertising, detergents replaced three-quarters of the market for soaps, much to the benefit of the makers of detergents. Yet this triumph of advertising could not have occurred in the absence of a prior need for a cleansing agent. Thus while the producer has a great deal to say about how wants are to be satisfied, the consumer has not been altogether silenced. Consumer sovereignty might best be regarded as a doctrine of limited monarchy rather than divine right, with the producer in the role of a very persuasive Prime Minister.

The theory of social balance

Galbraith writes that the concern of his essay "has been with the thralldom of a myth—the myth that the production of goods, by its overpowering importance and its ineluctable difficulty, is the central problem of our lives" (p. 250).

Under the spell of this myth, we have failed to ask what production is for. Having failed to ask, we have ended up with "an opulent supply of some things and a niggardly yield of others. This disparity carries to the point where it is a cause of social discomfort and social unhealth" (p. 221). What then are the reasons for this notorious imbalance?

1. *Want creation.* The most prominent cause of imbalance is that already discussed at length: the management of demand through advertising. The manufacturer of TV sets extolls the virtues of TV sets, for it is in his particular interest to do so. No one extolls the virtues of education, for the school board is not a private profit-seeking corporation and does not advertise. Consequently the advantages of privately sold goods are dinned into our ears; the advantages of public services are neglected; and we follow through by channeling our expenditures into TV sets and away from education.

2. *Growth.* Closely allied to our national preoccupation with marketable goods and the advertising of them is the official philosophy, previously noted, that the solution of social ills lies in the continued expansion of production. As the GNP gets bigger year by year, the funds for health, education, welfare and parks will get bigger too, and no special attention need be given them. The more GNP, the less poverty; the less poverty, the less need to be concerned with the public service sector. Some such reasoning lay behind the neglect of inequality as a public issue in the 50s and 60s.

3. *Inflation.* But inflation, which has been a crucial unsolved problem of the postwar period, makes the public services sector run faster just to stand still. Local services, such as schools, recreational facilities and municipal housekeeping are financed through property taxes which fall behind as the price level rises. Inflation erodes the tax base of cities and towns. The issue which Galbraith discussed in 1958 is now coming to a head in a taxpayers' revolt against further increases in local tax levies. Schools are forced to practice austerity as school budgets are voted down, and a national discussion is in

progress which questions whether property taxes are the right way to finance education in the first place.

4. *Military spending.* A large proportion of the federal budget is preempted for arms.

5. *Resource allocation.* Investment in bricks and mortar is private; investment in individuals (education and scientific training) is public. No market machinery allocates resources between the two because no profit is to be made from training even if the return to society is high. The result is not only an imbalance in resource allocation, but a further exacerbation of imbalance between the private and public sectors.

Now we must decide how much of Galbraith's argument about social imbalance is valid. When he wrote *The Affluent Society,* it was perhaps not so clear to everyone as it is today that there was in fact the social imbalance which Galbraith decries. *The Affluent Society* played no small part in bringing this issue to the attention of the educated public. But certain ambiguities in Galbraith's analysis, as well as his tendency to overstate certain points, opened him to attack. If we take the whole array of goods and services which a society requires, both private and public, and say that there is some reasonable order of priorities in which these goods and services should be produced so that we may achieve social balance, that, I assume, is a fairly clear statement. The difficulty begins if we say that there is a surfeit of things. Most people want more things, no matter how well off they are. If they have all the necessities, then they start wanting luxuries. If they have one painting, they may then want another one. By asserting that we produce so many goods that the corporations have to create the desire for the goods as well as the goods themselves, Galbraith gets himself into a debate on a subsidiary point. The issue ought not to be whether we have an overabundance of goods, but whether we have the right order of priorities in the production of goods and services. It is not the superabundance of electric toothbrushes and can openers in any absolute sense that need concern us, but rather the question of investing resources to make electric toothbrushes and can openers versus spending the resources to improve public education.

Another spurious problem is Galbraith's apparent disregard for efficiency. He is right that, with a high level of productivity, efficiency is not the principal problem. It is certainly preferable to have an economy with a high level of productivity based on scientific technology, run somewhat inefficiently, than to have a much less productive economy based on primitive technology, run very efficiently. But given the level of technology we have, it is obviously preferable, *ceteris paribus,* to have more efficiency rather than less. One obvious reason is that the more efficiently the goods producing sector runs, the more the labor and capital that can be spared for the services sector. Greater efficiency will give us more of both goods and services. Moreover, the dividing line between private goods and public services is not at all clear. In order to expand public services we need more of the physical plant in which they operate—principally housing, schools and hospitals.

In putting so much emphasis on advertising and financing as the mechanisms by which privately produced goods are favored above public services, Galbraith neglects to analyze the social milieu in which these mechanisms work.[4] The dominant values in America are the values of a profit-oriented system. Private production is motivated by profit and firms do what is profitable. The structure of privilege based on wealth reinforces the perpetuation of social imbalance. At the same time there are important national differences among capitalist industrial states. England, France and Sweden have achieved much better social balance than the United States. Their systems of welfare state measures are much more complete and satisfactory than ours. Yet they also have corporations that are profit-oriented and engage in advertising. They also have a wealthy upper class that benefits from these activities, but their histories differ from American history in various ways. The prominence of rugged individualism in the American conscience has meant that government actions are always suspect. No American class is imbued with a strong tradition of social responsibility. It is very hard to have an adequate system of social security when the belief prevails that every man ought to look out for himself and the devil take the hindmost.

The weakness of Galbraith's thesis is that he does not get deeply enough into the structural causes of social imbalance. His generalizations seem to be directed at industrial society as such but as soon as we make comparisons we see that they are limited to the United States. That being the case, it is necessary to go a step further

4. Although heaven knows that there has been plenty of advertising of social imbalance in the last fifteen years, all of it unpaid, and all of it to be found in the columns of the local newspaper. If advertising were the main problem, social balance today should be in an exemplary state.

and ask why there are different degrees of social imbalance in different capitalist countries.

We can illustrate what we mean by structural causes of social imbalance by borrowing a leaf from Charles H. Hession's book *John Kenneth Galbraith and His Critics*.[5] Hession rightly notes that much of the social imbalance of which Galbraith speaks can be ascribed to the great postwar migration of the middle class from the central cities to the suburbs, and of the rural poor into the cities. The consequence of those migrations is that the tax base of the cities is eroded; at the same time, because of failings in national economic policy, the cost of services is inflated. The cities are caught in a revenue-cost scissors from which there is no escape save by a restructuring of economic preferences which will divert resources to the cities. And at bottom that means nothing less than attacking inequality head on. This may seem a hopeless task until it is realized that the country as a whole cannot function without the cities as centers of commerce and the arts, and the cities cannot function if they slip into anarchy, as they are doing at present.

Program for the redress of balance

Galbraith discusses ways to remedy the poverty of public services. At present, the money is unavailable. But the solution lies in those taxes which automatically make

5. W. W. Norton & Co., Inc., 1972. Aside from its other merits, this book has a short biography of Galbraith, a complete catalogue of his books, and an extensive bibliography of reviews by friend and foe alike.

a pro rata share of increasing income available to public
authorities for public purposes. These are the personal
and corporate income taxes. They rise more than propor-
tionately with increases of private income. But they are
preempted in large measure by arms. In 1967 states and
localities spent 76 billion dollars of their own funds, excluding federal grants, which was about equal to spending for military and space. If an appreciable part of this
became available for civilian services of federal, state
and local governments, social balance could be quickly
restored. In Galbraith's view, liberals should resist tax reductions, even those that ostensibly favor the poor, if such
reductions are at the price of social balance. Galbraith
also advocates use of the sales tax despite its regressive-
ness. He contends that the sales tax is no longer a big
factor in the income of the poor and can be a ready
source of funds to supply the services needed to help
eliminate poverty. Moreover, the sales tax increases as
the value of goods and services sold increases. In contrast, the existing property tax for local services does not
automatically increase as gross national product increases, and as long as local services are financed on this
basis, they are bound to continue to be starved for funds.
I take it that Galbraith offers the sales tax as a program
of last resort, since there is a hint of pennypinching in ex-
pecting the poor to pay for their own emancipation
through taxes on their own purchases.

Possibly nothing else in *The Affluent Society* stirred
up as much controversy as Galbraith's discussion of poverty. The ire of critics was aroused by Galbraith's apparent underestimation of poverty and the apparent contradiction between pooh-poohing production and wanting at
the same time to eliminate poverty. In the first edition he

speaks of families with incomes below $1,000, or about one family in thirteen, as "the hard core of the very poor." Leon Keyserling, former Chairman of the Council of Economic Advisers, attacking Galbraith in the *New Republic* (October 27, 1958), gave statistics that placed about one-fifth of the nation in poverty and another fifth in deprivation. He saw no way of tackling poverty without increasing production and took Galbraith to task for thinking otherwise. There is no doubt that Galbraith cited figures which gave the impression that poor people were indeed a small minority; this impression he corrected in the second edition (1971), adopting figures within the twenty percent range. There is also no doubt that Galbraith's language—today poverty is "more nearly an afterthought"—justified the attack on him. That phrase is removed from the second edition, and an introduction has been added which contains a section protesting that one of the author's central concerns in writing *The Affluent Society* was precisely the question of poverty, as witnessed by the fact that in the early stages of writing he had in mind the title *Why People Are Poor*. The matter ought to be allowed to rest there, except to say that even socially aware liberals underestimated the extent of poverty in the 1950s.

Statistics notwithstanding, Galbraith's strength lay in the fact that he saw a direct connection between social imbalance and poverty. He distinguishes two kinds of poverty in contemporary America: case poverty, characterized by some deficiency in education, health or self-discipline (alcoholism, for example); and insular poverty, characterized by harsh conditions affecting whole islands of people such as those living in rural or urban slums. These kinds of poverty are not remedied by a general advance in income. Case poverty requires specific attention to specific individual inadequacies. Insular poverty requires assistance to the community from the outside. "Poverty is self-perpetuating because the poorest communities are poorest in the services which would eliminate it" (p. 294). And: "It will be clear that, to a remarkable extent, the remedy for poverty leads to the same requirements as those for social balance" (p. 295). We cannot get around the problem of cost. The search for deeper explanations of poverty is motivated by this hope.

These remarks certainly cannot be interpreted as a lack of concern over poverty. Nor can Galbraith's de-emphasis of production be so interpreted. Given the premise that we are sufficiently productive, the issue then is what we do with our productive capacity. We evade that issue if we concentrate on increasing production from year to year without respect to who benefits or how. But why must we be caught up in Galbraith's exasperating habit of stating problems in terms of either-or? One need not be opposed to a larger GNP in order to be concerned with its composition. Even if we don't need more fur-belows, a larger GNP will allow us to have more medical research than a smaller one, to take one example. But if Galbraith laid all the options before us with crystal clarity, nothing would be left for interpretation, and his works would go unnoticed by the critics.[6]

Galbraith concludes *The Affluent Society* by focusing his attention on what he calls the New Class, otherwise known as the educated middle class. Those who enter

6. Recently the author heard Galbraith say that he is in favor of increasing the GNP if the composition is right.

this class can avail themselves of easier and more pleasing work and shorter hours. Its members are more aware of social and political issues and are more articulate. The requirements of modern technology, administration and education have resulted in a burgeoning of the New Class; the continued, rapid expansion of this class should be a major social goal. Education is the operative factor. No one, I presume, can cavil with this advice, since a growing New Class equals a growing number of people with more income, leisure, education, articulateness, status, dignity and power. If, as the movies tell us, life in the New Class is boring and banal, it is nevertheless better to be bored and banal with a comfortable income than without one. One problem at a time. As Brecht once said, *Erst kommt das Fressen, und dann kommt die Moral,* which freely translated means, first we eat; then we chat about morality.

CHAPTER 4

The New Industrial State

MANY THICK BOOKS come into this world to demonstrate simple propositions which can be stated in a few words. *The New Industrial State* is such a book and the proposition is that the economic system should serve the people and not the reverse. A great investigatory superstructure is erected to prove that the economy imposes an irrational mode of life on the individual and that this need not be the case. Galbraith's work on the affluent society introduced the issue and the present book is a consummate effort to get to the bottom of it. The result is a painstaking examination of the great corporation and all its transcendent relations to the state and society.

The specifics of the analysis bring us to several untidy and difficult issues: planning versus the market; corporations and their purposes; consumer welfare; and the Midas partnership of business and government. We disagree with much of Galbraith's technical reasoning; we agree with many of his social inferences. This split in attitude is less perplexing than it seems. There is more than one route to the conclusion that corporate supremacy is an abomination and that pervasive commercialism is an evil. Travelers may disagree on why they have fallen into a bog yet agree on what efforts to make to get out of it.

Some reviewers profess to see a contradiction in Galbraith's admiration for the technical virtuosity of the large corporation and his detestation of the uses to which it is put. They overlook the fact that while Galbraith thinks the logic of industrial development makes large business inevitable, he also thinks that the same logic brings to life a countervailing power capable of domesticating this troublesome giant.

The industrial system and planning

Galbraith's intention is to construct a model which faithfully reflects the main features of twentieth-century industrial capitalism. Small and middle-sized enterprises are not characteristic; they typify an earlier period and so are excluded. Today the industrial system is dominated by five or six hundred corporations which have unique attributes: they have passed beyond the entrepreneurial stage; they commonly share an industry with three or four others; they have emancipated themselves from the market; they are run by a technical elite; and they seek objectives other than profit maximization.

These organizational entities are called mature corporations to distinguish them from entrepreneurial corporations. The mature corporation did not appear on the scene by chance. It evolved as an instrument for dealing with the intricacies of technology and the market. In the entrepreneurial stage, things were simpler. The first Ford, to use Galbraith's illustration, was produced in a small plant in a short time without much planning. Now production is quite a different matter. To get the Mustang from the drawing board to the road required years of preparation; the application of expert knowledge; a division of tasks into their component parts; a large amount of capital; a precise definition of the way in which the job was to be done; specialized manpower and sophisticated organization. In a word, planning.

A firm subject to such constraints must control inputs and outputs. It must ensure that the necessary supplies of labor, materials and equipment are on hand at the right prices. And it must see to it that the consumer buys what the firm thinks he is going to buy at prices and in quantities contemplated beforehand. As Galbraith puts it, the firm "must exercise control over what is sold. It must exercise control over what is supplied." And here is his crucial observation: "It must replace the market with planning" (p. 23).

To aver that the firm replaces the market with planning is no trivial claim. Until the appearance of *The New Industrial State,* economists had unanimously agreed that all firms in a capitalist economy, even monopolies, operate in a market. The market is the form of organization which exists—by definition—when buying and selling occur. Galbraith, stressing that the mature corporation takes the initiative in its relations with suppliers and customers, and does business as much as possible on its own terms—indeed on terms planned by its staff well in advance—asserts that the market has been supplanted.

The difficulty with this far-reaching thesis is that it glosses over the distinction between planning as that term is used to refer to the activities of an individual enterprise and planning as it refers to the activities of an entire economy. To say that each enterprise plans is not to imply that there is an overall plan for all enterprises. Irving Kristol made the point quite aptly when he observed that a poker game in which each player plans his moves as carefully as possible is not the same as one in which a single person plans the moves of all the players.[1] Planning does not replace the market unless the activities of enterprises are coordinated from one center in accordance with one internally consistent budget. An oligopolistic firm is able to influence the terms and conditions of purchase and sale; it still functions in a market. There is a vast difference between stabilizing market influences and removing them altogether. Galbraith's treatment skirts this vital distinction. The difference between the U.S. and Soviet economies is reduced to a blur.

The market and attendant price mechanism (however imperfect) are rejected; no satisfactory explanation relating the plans of one firm to those of others is forthcoming: Galbraith alas is left without a theory of economic organization.[2]

1. *Fortune,* July 1967.
2. I am indebted to a review by Scott Gordon for this point. "The Close of the Galbraithian System," *Journal of Political Economy,* July-August 1968. In a reply to Gordon, Galbraith wrote: "But these efforts [of the firm to plan] operate against the similar efforts of other firms—a process I have sketched although far from fully described—and against the increasing market resistance of the consumers and the increasing cost (as Professor Gordon rightly observes) of a given increment of sales. These are the constraints. They would not exist with total producer sovereignty, but they do with lesser producer power. And this, in turn, is a very different world from that of consumer sovereignty." *Journal of Political Economy,* July-August 1969,

45

Economies and diseconomies of scale

Galbraith's claims for the advantages of size are succinctly reflected in two characteristic remarks: "General Motors is not only large enough to afford the best size of automobile plant but is large enough to afford a dozen or more of the best size" (p. 76). And: "The size of General Motors is in the service not of monopoly or the economies of scale but of planning. And for this planning—control of supply, control of demand, provision of capital, minimization of risk—there is no clear upper limit to the desirable size" (p. 76).

Some benefits of size are obvious: the ability to afford and to manage large-scale R&D operations; sufficient assets to buy the best management and staff know-how; economies in advertising and distribution; ease in borrowing; and of course control over the many variables which Galbraith subsumes under planning.

There are items on the debit side, however, and these have been forcefully stated by one of Galbraith's long-standing adversaries, Walter Adams.[3] Adams argues that Galbraith has failed to show that "Brobdingnagian size" is necessary for efficiency, technological progress and effective planning in the public interest. Optimum plant size in many industries is getting smaller because of the

p. 501. These welcome comments lead inescapably to the conclusion that planning has not replaced the market and to the further conclusion that no one has understood *The New Industrial State*.

3. "Planning, Regulation and Competition," in *Hearings before Subcommittees of the Select Committee on Small Business*, Government Printing Office, 1967.

characteristics of new technology. Nevertheless the super-corporations are getting larger and usually operate many plants. The breakup of industrial giants would in no way diminish the efficiency of production but, in fact, would enhance it through the elimination of excessive corporate bureaucracy. Neither is large size necessary for innovations; most innovations were cultivated by small and middle-sized firms and taken over for production and marketing by large ones only when their value had already been demonstrated. Finally, large firms may plan in their own interests and enhance their own power and ability to make profits, but it does not follow that such planning is in the public interest. Indeed as competition declines prices go up, quality goes down and the public suffers. Giantism is in the service of privilege, not technology. Moreover, much swollen size is accounted for not by the requirements of technology or planning, but by government actions which nullify the efforts of the antitrust division of the Justice Department. The government abets size and privilege in the way it awards defense contracts, allocates research and development support, and through patent policy, tax privileges, stockpiling arrangements, tariffs and subsidies.

Partisan arguments aside, it is pointless either to attack or to defend large size across the board. Galbraith ignores studies showing that most postwar inventions were made outside the laboratories of giant corporations. At the same time he is right that the development of much contemporary technology depends on the resources of super-large corporations working hand in hand with government. An example from the steel industry illustrates the first point: the oxygen furnace was invented and put into operation in a miniscule firm in Austria. But at the other extreme, industries such as aerospace and atomic energy require more capital than even the largest firms can command and they must rely on the federal government to underwrite the costs of development.

Galbraith readily admits that the price of bigness is a loss of efficiency. This does not worry him since it is more than made up by superior productivity.[4] The Russians once thought so too; perhaps an interesting lesson can be learned from their mistakes. The planners read *Das Kapital* and found that concentration and centralization were taking place in the West. Somehow they saw in this the wave of the future. So they built big. The result was that every plant had to be self-sufficient and make its own tools, spare parts and countless other items. There followed administrative headaches for which not even Stalin could find relief short of removing the head. In recent years Soviet economists have arrived at a more balanced view. They finally noticed that the U.S. economy has not only a few hundred big businesses but also a multitude of small and middle-sized ones. They observed that large firms like GM and GE subcontract with hundreds of suppliers that specialize in small runs and one-of-a-kind products. The Russians saw the light. They recognized that the best slogan isn't always the bigger the better! They belatedly and painfully acknowledged that

4. To recapitulate the argument: the larger enterprise is better able to survive the depredations of competition and the fluctuations of the market than the small enterprise, and therefore is better able to take advantage of superior productivity. Given two enterprises with the same level of productivity, the larger is more likely to be around in the long run.

there is no single optimum firm size for all purposes. *Nomine mutato, de te fabula narratur.*[5]

The technostructure

Who runs the corporation? The conventional answer is management. Galbraith's answer is the technostructure. And what is the technostructure? In Galbraith's words, it "extends from the most senior officials of the corporation to where it meets, at the outer perimeter, the white and blue collar workers whose function is to conform more or less mechanically to instruction or routine. It embraces all who bring specialized knowledge, talent or experience to group decision-making. This, not the management, is the guiding intelligence—the brain—of the enterprise" (pp. 70-71).

Since no single person is master of all the expert knowledge needed in the course of business, decision-making is necessarily a function of groups. That being the case, Galbraith reasons that "when power is exercised by a group not only does it pass over into the organization but it passes irrevocably." He continues: "If the decision required the combined information of a group, it cannot be safely reversed by an individual. He will have to get the judgment of other specialists. This returns the power once more to organization" (pp. 65-66). In short, "Effec-

5. See the article by Ia. B. Kvasha in *Production, Accumulation and Consumption,* International Arts & Sciences Press, Inc., 1967. The quote from Horace can be rendered: Change the name, and the tale is told about you.

tive power of decision is lodged deeply in the technical, planning and other specialized staff" (p. 68).

If the point is valid, why not dispense with the management of the 500 largest corporations altogether? The mere ratification of proposals which bubble up to the executive suites out of the wisdom of the technostructure is only ceremonial, like the announcement of government policies by the queen. But there is one proviso: "leadership assigns tasks to committees from which decisions emerge . . . it selects the men who comprise the groups that make the decisions, and it constitutes and reconstitutes these groups in accordance with changing need. This is, perhaps, its [management's] most important function" (p. 69). Doesn't this apparently modest concession to management spoil the whole case? If the person who seeks power has to choose between making decisions subject to approval or having approval over those who make decisions, he will elect the latter without hesitation. For the power to pick the group which makes decisions is tantamount to having the power to get the decisions one wants, and the power of the technostructure disappears.

But that is not all. An orchestra must have a conductor who conducts, an army must have a commander who commands, and a corporation (even a mature corporation) must have a management that manages. Management supplies organization; it supplies coordination; it supplies consistent goals; it supplies decision-making in emergencies; it supplies crucial decisions in expansion and diversification; it resolves problems when experts give conflicting advice. Certainly in performing these functions management must rely on competent technical advice. But Galbraith confuses the technical complexity which requires the attention of engineers, computer experts, tax specialists, accountants and advertising professionals with the strategic business decisions which have to be made in light of technical information. Management decisions concerning profit and losses, expansion and retrenchment, specialization and diversification, internal and external financing, domestic and overseas investment, and hiring and firing of key staff members are different in quality from technical decisions having to do with the kind of alloy to use in a jet plane, the best components for a computer, or the writing of an effective TV commercial.

Corporate decision-making is not a closed-loop feedback process with management as a mere conduit of decisions which emerge from the guts of the technostructure and pass back to it automatically. In the real world things happen quite differently. The executive is active, not passive. His function is to provide organization, to change it where necessary, to create it where it is needed and none exists. In Robin Marris' words " . . . the testing tasks of business life are those which are the least routine." The manager is a doer. "In order to demonstrate ability he must develop new markets, increase his share of old ones, develop new methods of production, organize a merger or at least do *something*."[6]

Looking through *Fortune* or *Business Week* we find innumerable examples of the uses of corporate power. When new management replaces the old; when corporations are in crisis; when they embark on dramatic new ventures: then the dominant role of management be-

6. *The Economic Theory of "Managerial" Capitalism,* pp. 58 and 59.

comes obvious. After Harold Geneen became President of ITT in 1959, that company launched a program of acquisitions which made it the twenty-first largest industrial corporation in sales ($2.8 billion) and the nineteenth largest in assets ($3 billion).[7] Was it merely coincidence that ITT's technostructure decided to take the path of conglomerate expansion at the very moment that Geneen became company president? When T. Vincent Learson succeeded Thomas J. Watson, Jr. as President of IBM, Learson (or was it the technostructure?) reorganized top management, returning to an alignment that separates manufacturing from sales and service operations all the way through to the corporate office level.[8] Why did the IBM technostructure wait for Learson to become president before it made this move? It is hard to suppress the suspicion that it was Learson himself who made the change.

When Richard C. Gerstenberg became Chairman of General Motors, that company switched to the concept of a collective top management which shared responsibility for directing GM.[9] Did this decision come out of the bowels of the technostructure or did Gerstenberg and other top officials institute it? The same article mentions that the hallowed management system inaugurated by Alfred P. Sloan, Jr. had come under criticism. Among other things, Sloan cultivated top management within the ranks of GM. Recently the company recruited four key

7. I am indebted to a review of *The New Industrial State,* Second Edition, by Eli Goldston in *Business and Society Review,* Spring 1972, for this illustration.

8. *Business Week,* January 22, 1972.

9. *Business Week,* December 11, 1971.

executives from outside. Former President James Roche is quoted (in his best prose) as saying "In some instances, perhaps people were able to develop an expertise in some of these things that are concerning us now to better advantage on the outside than on the inside." For good measure, the article quotes a former GM public relations executive: "Once I had an assignment to go out to the tech center and review major breakthroughs in research. I found out there weren't any." The anecdote is not idiosyncratic, since, as we found, most research, invention and development take place outside the large corporation. To be strictly logical we would have to say that most of the technostructure also exists outside the large corporation. The implications for a theory of business management are highly irregular.

Nothing reveals management's authority more than mismanagement. Its errors of omission and commission, if sizable enough, can convulse the hugest organization, and the faithful technostructure availeth nothing. All doubts will certainly be put to rest if the reader consults *Corporations in Crisis,* a compendium of lurid details about unfortunate episodes in the history of Olin Mathieson, General Dynamics, General Electric, U.S. Steel, Boeing and more.[10]

The goals of the industrial system

No one ever doubted what made the competitive system tick: it was the drive for profit maximization. The

10. *Corporations in Crisis* by Richard Austin Smith, Doubleday, 1963.

striving for maximum profits was not just a personal pen-
chant of entrepreneurs; it was a necessity imposed on
them by the rigors of competition. Profits meant accumulation of capital; accumulation of capital meant competitive strength; competitive strength meant survival. Those
who fell too far behind in the perpetual quest for profits
had to drop out of the race. With the first frost of depression, a sudden change in market conditions, or the intro-
duction of a new competitive product, the weak ones
went to the wall. Every businessman could agree with
Marx, assuming he had heard the phrase: Accumulate,
accumulate: that is Moses and the Prophets!

Such compulsion operated in the laissez-faire economy
in the bad old days and prevails in the entrepreneurial
part of the economy today. But the mature corporation is
a different species and has different goals, according to
Galbraith. It seeks not maximum but minimum profits.
This amazing turnabout occurred after management assumed control of the corporation, a development described in *The Modern Corporation and Private Property,* published in 1932 by A. A. Berle and Gardner
Means. Ownership and control of the large corporation
—most large corporations, at any rate—became separate
and distinct; stock ownership was dispersed among nu-
merous asset holders, any one holding being too small
to control the corporation; management passed from
the hands of the Master Builders-Owners—Rockefeller,
Morgan, Harriman, Hartford and the like—into the
hands of a group of professional managers who did not
themselves own the corporation. Galbraith takes the process a step further. Power has passed from the managers
to the technostructure. The stockholders may indeed still
want to maximize profits; but since the managers, and

most certainly the technostructure, are a different set of people from the stockholders, the wishes of the latter need not be the wishes of the former. Galbraith heaps scorn on the absurd proposition that the managers obtain vicarious pleasure from their alleged efforts to enrich the stockholders. To use his colorful simile, this is somewhat like saying that the sexual desires of the stockholders drive the managers to frenzied activity. Not so. The technostructure has sexual interests of its own.

These are above all survival of the technostructure (and with it the corporation) and decision-making autonomy. Survival requires avoidance of unnecessary risks but minimum earnings which are large enough to keep stockholders happy and to generate an internal supply of savings for investment. Failing these two goals, stockholders will become restive and start thinking about prying into the internal affairs of the corporation; the corporation will also jeopardize its independence by having to apply to outsiders for capital.

After having secured its autonomy by a minimum level of earnings, the next most important goal of the technostructure is to achieve the greatest possible rate of growth. An expanding output means an expanding technostructure, more jobs, more responsibility, more promotions, more compensation. Growth is consistent with the personal and pecuniary interests of the technostructure and with the paramount public policy of expanding the gross national product and underwriting employment. The technostructure-corporation then is free to pursue other goals such as technological virtuosity, corporate responsibility or giving money to the Girl Scouts.[11]

11. Here, in passing, let us briefly mention Galbraith's dubious

Galbraith's theorem of corporate goals is buttressed by a very neat classification of motivation—one that is completely irrevelant. He distinguishes four types of motivation which induce people to work: compulsion; money; identification with goals superior to one's own; and adaptation, or the hope of making the goals of an organization more in accord with one's own. In a market economy, compulsion is ruled out and pecuniary motivation is universal. But after a person has reached a certain level of income and influence in the corporate structure, identification and adaptation take over as the main motives. The closer one gets to the top, the more important adaptation becomes. While in fact those in the upper reaches of the technostructure may get personal satisfaction from influencing the goals of the corporation and those in lower levels may experience a pleasant feeling of identification in being associated with an organization that presumably is doing something important, and while the lowly production workers may have to extract their main satisfaction from a weekly paycheck, all these perfectly genuine personal satisfactions have next to nothing to do with the goals of the corporation.

The difficulty is that Galbraith sees corporate goals as being defined from within the corporation, subject to the motivations of the technostructure, while in reality, the goals of the corporation are determined from without.

> Principle of Consistency, which alleges that the goals of the corporation correspond to the goals of society. So it appears when one thinks of growth, technology, the production of gadgets and a rising standard of living. But apparently a new principle must be invoked—the Principle of Inconsistency—when one thinks of supersonic jets, mercury in fish and carbon monoxide in the air.

Just as profit maximization, the goal of an enterprise in a competitive market, is imposed on it by the very nature of competition, regardless of whether the entrepreneur is a power-mad megalomaniac or a kindly patriarch who loves children and his pet dog, so the goals of the so-called mature corporation are imposed on it by its external environment regardless of the personal motivations of the technostructure, including top management. If planning and the market are mutually exclusive, the market and its influences vanish; but if the market is restored to its rightful place and oligopolies compete with one another, then the external discipline of the market is re-introduced. That external discipline means that a firm is obliged to accumulate in order to survive the rigors of competition. Oligopolistic competition implies some combination of profit maximization and growth. For the firm which is content with minimum profits certainly cannot grow, much less survive. It is difficult to see how maximum growth, acknowledged by Galbraith as a decisive goal of the corporation, can be reconciled with minimum profits. Moreover, it is rather awkward to say that the competitive firm is compelled to maximize its profits while the oligopolistic firm is only required to obtain a minimum: it is odd to encounter a theory in which minimum means more than maximum. Minimum earnings are not sufficient to compete successfully. The firm is compelled to grow not because of the subjective desires of the technostructure, but because of competition. It will lose out in the race (and may be subject to a takeover bid) just as a competitive firm will if it fails to grow, but a fast rate of growth is contingent upon a high rate of earnings. Accumulation of capital, growth and profits are different ways of looking at the same thing.

Perhaps one difficulty is that the parties to the dispute over profit maximization—and this is a dispute which has been raging in the economics profession for several decades—are talking past one another. Adolph Lowe made the ingenious observation in his book *On Economic Knowledge* that the tacit assumption of classical and neoclassical economics is that profit maximization takes place in the short run. Given the institutional setting prevalent when the theory of the firm was being elaborated in the nineteenth century, the short-run assumption made sense. It is not compatible with the modern industrial regime in which profits must be considered in a long-run context, the length of the run depending on a diversity of technological and organizational considerations. In an oligopolistic system, therefore, no general maximization rule applies to all industries and all firms. Profit maximization is compatible with different kinds of behavior according to expectations concerning demand, supply and price. As Lowe puts it, the extremum principle (maximization in this case) has lost its predictive reliability. Hence—and this point is mine—the compatibility of various strategies with the search for profit maximization; the issue is not motivation but the time horizon over which profits are calculated.

It is easy to make absurd statements about maximization or the lack of it. The maximum rate of growth, without any qualifications, means that the firm will overextend itself, use up its capital resources and end up undercapitalized. Or it may use up its personnel and end up with an overextended management and technostructure. A sensible conception of maximization means maximization within the constraints imposed by the necessity of operating a going concern. Within those constraints, management maximizes profits and growth by striking a balance between them—here there is room for policy differences—and not by sacrificing one to the other. Growth after all means larger net earnings later, and the problem which obfuscates this whole area of discourse is how much later is later.

Profit maximization may be a little fuzzy around the edges, but, as Robert Solow has pointed out, it is not only possible to live with the fuzziness but necessary. "Does the modern industrial corporation maximize profits? Probably not rigorously and singlemindedly, and for much the same reason that Dr. Johnson did not become a philosopher—because cheerfulness keeps breaking in. . . ." But the received doctrine "can survive if businesses merely *almost* maximize profits. The real question is whether there is some other goal that businesses pursue systematically at the expense of profits." The common view is that "a corporation will seek the largest possible profits in some appropriately long-run sense, and with due allowance for cheerfulness."[12] Profit maximization is an example of what Benjamin Ward calls a stylized fact. A stylized fact is not the literal truth, but it is close enough to the truth to be accepted as if it were. What appears to be an anomaly to some economists is, so it seems, a belated discovery that economics has been working with a stylized fact for 150 years without realizing it.

12. "The New Industrial State or Son of Affluence," *The Public Interest,* Fall 1967, p. 106. Even assuming growth maximization instead of profit maximization, and assuming a list of projects with the same degree of risk, management will choose the one which appears to promise the highest rate of profit.

Some institutional considerations also reinforce the notion that profit maximization is not to be dismissed as a relic of the past. To begin with, a study by Robert J. Lampman indicates that 1.6 percent of the population owns at least 80 percent of the corporate stock.[13] Another study by G. William Domhoff informs us that this upper stratum of wealth-holders contains within it a pool of talent from which a disproportionate number of corporate directors is recruited.[14] This wealthy upper class circle has common ties through schools, colleges, clubs and intermarrying families, not to mention a common interest in money. There may be a separation of ownership from control when it comes to the tens of thousands of small stockholders, but this is not the case with regard to the very wealthy.

A study by Robert J. Larner on "The Effect of Management-control on the Profits of Large Corporations," in which he compares 128 management-controlled corporations with 59 owner-controlled ones, all among the top 500, calls to our notice that management-controlled firms earned profits only one-half of one percent lower than owner-controlled firms, showing that both types of cor-

---

13. *The Share of Top Wealth-holders in National Wealth, 1922-1956,* Princeton University Press, 1962.

14. *Who Rules America?* Prentice-Hall, Inc., 1967. Domhoff's study of corporate directors shows that in the top 15 banks, 15 insurance companies and 20 industrials, 53 percent of the 884 leading men were (in 1963) members of the upper class. The other 47 percent were individuals who had gotten the message about the singular benefits of profits and who were themselves in various stages of pecuniary assimilation into the upper class.

poration are similarly profit-oriented.[15] His study also found that, of 93 executives of the corporations studied, 41 owned stock exceeding one million dollars in market value and that the compensation of the 93 chief executives depended primarily on the corporations' dollar profits and rate of return on equity. Thus the executives' and the stockholders' interest in profitability substantially overlap.

Finally, a study by Robert Sheehan questions the common assumption that management control is all but universal among large corporations.[16] Sheehan found that 150 companies of the 500 largest industrials were controlled by an individual or by members of a single family. His criterion for control was ownership of at least 10 percent of a company's voting stock, an extremely conservative standard, which for instance excludes Richard K. Mellon, the largest stockholder in Alcoa (2.98 percent) and in Gulf Oil (1.78 percent) and the second largest stockholder among GM directors (.084 percent). The Patman Committee's criterion for control is 5 percent, in which case the number of large corporations controlled by individuals or families is higher than the figure given by Sheehan.

These data suggest the conclusion that there is not very much difference in the conduct of so-called management-controlled and owner-controlled firms. The demise

15. In *American Society, Inc.,* edited by Maurice Zeitlin, Markham Publishing Company, 1970. This compendium for critics is not the same book as *America, Inc.,* referred to earlier, although the authors have obviously had a similar inspiration.
16. Ibid.

of the proprietary firm has been greatly exaggerated and those firms which are management-controlled are not free from the preponderant influence of wealthy individuals who sit on corporate boards and exercise a powerful influence from within. Paul Sweezy hits the mark with breathtaking precision—managers are functionaries of capital. That phrase epitomizes the role of the manager. His actions as a manager are not a function of his personal motives. Naturally he would not be a manager without personal motives. But those motives must conform to his function as a representative of capital. He represents a corporation which competes in and must grow in a market. He represents a concentrated ownership whose principal interest is to preserve and expand its capital and which will replace him if he doesn't make good. And he represents himself—management—the largest owner of corporate stock of any occupational group in the country. The functionary of capital does not choose his goals; they are goals imposed by the imperatives of the capitalist industrial system. They are embedded in the prevailing ideology; they are embraced by the public.

The revised sequence

We return to one of Galbraith's favorite vexations—the management of the consumer. In *The New Industrial State* the subject is treated as a vital part of corporate planning. The term revised sequence is used to emphasize the contrast with the sequence accepted by traditional economic theory: a unidirectional flow of instructions from the consumer through the market to the producer, otherwise known as consumer sovereignty. We met the same problem in *The Affluent Society* under the heading dependence effect. As before, Galbraith stresses that advertising is a device for managing consumer demand which in effect shifts the decision to purchase goods from the consumer to the firm. In *The New Industrial State,* however, he makes a sensible qualification: "This transfer, like the control of prices, is by no means complete" (p. 206). In the present treatment, Galbraith has much more to say about consumer testing and other forms of market research. The producer has to find out what the consumer wants before he goes about trying to make the consumer want it.

Conventional theory regards advertising of largely similar products by oligopolies as a form of wasteful competition which expands on essentially trivial differences between products A and B. Advertising budgets virtually cancel each other out. "Firms spend money to take business away from each other; all cannot succeed so the result is a standoff" (p. 205).

To Galbraith, this is nonsense. Advertising increases the flow of revenue to all who advertise. It gives firms a decisive influence over the revenues they receive. People buy more cars with advertising than without advertising. They choose cars as a mode of transportation as opposed to buses and trains. Advertising affects the direction of investment. It ensures that investment will be made in the automobile industry rather than in public transportation. It makes possible accelerated obsolescence. The clincher is this: "Were there but one manufacturer of automobiles in the United States, it would still be essential that it enter extensively on the management of its demand. Otherwise consumers, exercising the sovereignty that would be inconsistent with the company's planning, might resort to other forms of transportation and other ways of spending their income. This is the answer to the orthodox contention that advertising is principally induced by market oligopolies" (pp. 207-208).[17]

These observations are convincing up to a point, particularly since they are more restrained than earlier ones. But it is impossible to believe that the distribution of resources between cars and public transportation, for example, is determined exclusively by advertising. Auto manufacturers advertise in England, France and Japan almost as stridently as they do in the U.S., but the public transportation systems of those countries are embarrassingly superior to ours. The explanation must lie not exclusively in advertising, but in broad social attitudes, the causes of which lie outside the realm of Galbraith's analysis.

The management of demand is crucial in Galbraith's theory of industrial society, as we found in reviewing *The Affluent Society*. If demand is subject to manipulation, there is no reason to believe that the array of goods sold results in optimum consumer satisfaction; the case for letting the consumer and the producer work things out between themselves evaporates. "It is not the individual's right to buy that is being protected. Rather it is the seller's right to manage the individual" (p. 219). If this momentous conclusion sounds bland today, Galbraith's strenuous effort to win the field from the upholders of

17. Why couldn't advertising serve the dual purpose of insurance against substitutes, essential to monopolies and oligopolies alike, and insurance against loss of revenue to competing producers, essential only to oligopolies?

Simon-pure consumer sovereignty has something to do with it.

But Galbraith has a fresh point to make: the mature corporation sells more than commodities—it sells a way of life. Advertising helps develop the kind of person the industrial system requires, "one that reliably spends his income and works reliably because he is always in need of more. . . . Advertising by making goods important makes the industrial system important." A most significant observation follows: " . . . the technostructure would soon sink into the background were the supply of industrial products to become routine in the manner of water from a water works in a year of adequate rainfall. This would have happened long since had not advertising, with its unremitting emphasis on the importance of goods, kept people persuaded to the contrary" (p. 211).

Two strands of thought are tied together here and we shall have to try to separate them. On the technical side, productivity increases from year to year, a smaller part of the labor force engages in industrial production, and in a sense it is easier for society to supply itself with the stream of goods it consumes. It ought to be possible for industrial production to become an increasingly unobtrusive part of social life, leaving most of us to attend to other things. On the social side, however, the industrial system is highly concentrated, wields enormous power, is supported by values which are widely accepted and is tied through money and prestige to a class (the wealthy) and a stratum (the managers) whose privileges are indissolubly linked to that system. Advertising is simply one manifestation of the whole setup. Considering the technical side, business need not dominate our lives. But with regard to class, status and power, new social values and alignments are the crux of the matter, and advertising pales, if not into insignificance, at least into proper perspective.

The industrial system and the state

The mature corporation is inconceivable in isolation; it subsists in symbiosis with the state. The state supplements and completes the planning apparatus delineated in Galbraith's model. The centralized regulation of aggregate demand has become a commonly accepted practice of the new industrial state. But its planning responsibilities do not stop there. The rounding out of the model also requires that the state support the development of technology, control unemployment and inflation, share the process of decision-making with the mature corporation, provide planning where the market fails and act as guardian of the community's aesthetic needs.

The state and technology. Galbraith views military expenditures not only as a consequence of the East-West conflict but almost equally as an accommodation to the needs of the industrial system and technostructure. A corollary of military production is the underwriting of sophisticated technology on a grand scale. As the cold war fades and the public becomes disenchanted with overkill, nonlethal surrogates for military spending must be found which include similarly challenging projects for research and development. In his desire to be practical, Galbraith considered aerospace to be the best candidate. It is a sop to the vested interests and a means of employing engineers. But in recent years, the common sense of putting technicians to work on problems of health, transportation and pollution and on rational ways of organizing urban life has become increasingly apparent to the public, and Galbraith in subsequent manifestations has endorsed this more varied program.

Unemployment and inflation. Full employment and price stability are both essential to the smooth working of the industrial system and of Galbraith's model. Even with adequate demand, a residue of unemployment will persist because there is no match between the education and skills required in a sophisticated economy and those available among the unskilled unemployed. In Galbraith's view, education is "the difference that divides." This clearly is the case; but even engineers can lose their jobs, which suggests that although training and retraining are a necessary condition for the elimination of unemployment, they are not sufficient. The job slots must be made available for people to fill. In recent years, Galbraith has made the logical commitment and endorsed a public employment program.

The second requirement is to control the wage-price spiral. Galbraith emerges as something of a prophet here, since his was a lonely voice for controls a long time before they were applied. The revised edition of *The New Industrial State* was published just prior to the institution of the ninety-day wage-price freeze of the Nixon Administration. Galbraith wrote with considerable prescience: "While there may be further difficulties, and further failures or retreats, a system of wage and price control is inevitable in the industrial system. . . . Neither inflation nor unemployment is an acceptable alternative" (p. 260).

Indeed Galbraith's discussion of inflation in *The New Industrial State* makes up for an important omission in

The Affluent Society, in which he discussed only de-mand-pull inflation, inflation caused by an excess of de-mand over supply. The kind of inflation which plagued us in the late 50s and again (in part) in the late 60s was administered inflation, that is, inflation of wages and prices in the concentrated sector of the economy occur-ring simultaneously with inadequate demand and a high level of unemployment and unused capacity.[18] The di-lemma of public policy under such circumstances is that monetary and fiscal efforts to curtail rising prices only make unemployment and unused capacity greater; while efforts to stimulate the economy in order to increase em-ployment and the use of industrial capacity only cause greater inflation. Since such cost-push inflation originates in the concentrated sector, the obvious solution, which Galbraith has championed for many years, is to combine fiscal stimulus to bring demand to an adequate level with wage-price controls to arrest the inflationary spiral. In Galbraith's view, these controls need apply primarily to the small number of large corporations and unions which have the power to administer their prices and wages. In the nonconcentrated part of the economy, where firms and workers have only slight control over prices and wages, the state of demand and supply is the key. There is no need to have detailed wage-price administration over this sector. However, in cases where there are bottle-

18. However, the wage-price spiral of the late 60s and early 70s was brought about by egregious errors in the fiscal and mon-etary areas at the onset of heavy involvement in the Vietnam War (1965). The economy suffered from excess demand and liquidity which pushed up the price level and in turn started the wage-price leapfrog.

necks—medical service is a notorious example—special policies are required to ensure that the necessary facilities and trained manpower are forthcoming.

Since the publication of *The New Industrial State,* the inflation discussion has turned to the subject of productivity. The theme is that wage increases must be offset by productivity increases if inflation is to be avoided. The growing services sector is a particular worry to some economists because, as they point out, a barber cannot cut more than so many heads of hair an hour and a fiddler cannot increase his productivity by fiddling faster. But barbers and fiddlers (personal services) are only a small part of the general services sector, which includes government, trade, finance, communications, transportation, education and medical care. It strains credulity to lump so many disparate fields together but, be that as it may, many methods are available for increasing productivity in most of the services, including automatic data processing, economies of scale, standardization, specialization and better organization. The deliberate encouragement of productivity growth must now be added to the repertoire of anti-inflation policies.[19]

The state-industrial complex. No one doubts that the mature corporation and the state work on the most familiar terms. As Galbraith says, "No sharp line separates government from the private firm; the line becomes very indistinct and even imaginary. Each organization is important to the other; members are intermingled in daily work; each organization comes to accept the other's

---

19. The connection between productivity and inflation is explored at some length in *Business Week*, September 9, 1972.

goals; each adapts the goals of the other to its own. Each organization, accordingly, is an extension of the other . . . shared goals are the decisive link in each case" (p. 316).

This sharing of decision-making is particularly vivid in the handling of military business. The military-industrial complex actually is a complex in which the line between public and private cannot be drawn. The Department of Defense is engaged in management and the military firms are engaged in public policy-making by virtue of the DOD's dependence on the kinds of hardware available. Pervasive mutual influence takes place between nonmilitary industries and the government as well through circulating personnel, policy discussions and the need of each side to take the moves of the other into account. No doubt General Motors, General Electric and Standard Oil are affected with the public interest. But Galbraith, caught in a frequent failing, insists on either-or. Either the largest corporations are an extension of the state and part of one unified planning system or they are not. In asserting that they are, Galbraith effaces the important fact that powerful private corporations, though on intimate terms with the state, though sharing informal procedures of planning with the state and though public in the sense of having an enormous public influence, are still private institutions—privately owned, privately managed, and dedicated to the private purpose of making a profit. Whether we call industry public or private is a mere formality, judging by Galbraith's treatment of the subject. But there is institutional substance to that distinction which deeply affects the way industry is run and the nature of state-industry relations. The emphasis on technicalities explains Galbraith's exaggeration of the degree of convergence between the U.S. and Soviet economies. However, it has not prevented him in later writings from advocating the nationalization of certain industries such as the railroads where private enterprise has been a failure.

The planning lacunae. These pockets of failure in the private sector, where the market does not work and where, for whatever reason, the mature corporation has not stepped in, will eventually have to be absorbed into the planning structure of the state. Urban and interurban transportation, housing and land use are obvious candidates for a strong public planning and development authority. When the public becomes sufficiently extricated from the toils of market mythology to permit these sectors to be managed in a sane and businesslike way, the construction of the new industrial state will have been completed and the logic of the Galbraithian model fully realized.

The aesthetic dimension. This phrase refers to subjects now discussed under the headings of ecology and environment. Galbraith wrote before the current stir over corporate responsibility, and thought at the time that these issues were of no concern to the technostructure (which is interested in technology, not beauty). "Where there is a conflict between industrial and aesthetic priorities, it is the state which must assert aesthetic priority against the industrial need. Only the state can defend a landscape against power lines, advertisers, lumbermen, coal miners, and, on frequent occasions, its own highwaymen" (p. 352). Whether this division of labor between the mature corporation and the state holds up depends a great deal on the climate of opinion, and this brings us to our last subject. The new industrial state follows a definite trajectory which takes us in the direction of technical excellence but bypasses much which is desirable for a better life. What political forces are available to steer a new course?

Sources of political change

It would not be far from the mark to say that Galbraith has so painstakingly described the industrial system in order to denounce it. He does not propose to replace it with something else. He would have society use the industrial system rather than have the industrial system use society. His proposition that the intelligentsia is a force able to lead this change has been greeted by a certain amount of skepticism. But Galbraith is in good company. Everybody from Plato to Lenin has draped the mantle of leadership on the intellectuals and regarded them as carriers of one sort of ideal or another. Why should Galbraith be an exception?

In his view the industrial unions cannot be regarded as agents of reform because they have become part of the establishment and contributors to the planning system. Their absorption has been assisted by the readiness of large corporations to grant wage increases and pass them on to the consumer; by the public policy of high employment and high incomes; and by the decline in the proportion of blue-collar workers employed in industry and the corresponding increase in white-collar workers who have a greater feeling of identity with "their" corporation. The unions have accordingly shed their old functions and taken on new ones. They help to frame the rules and operate the grievance machinery; standardize wage costs; and ensure that increases occur at the same time throughout a given industry. They enjoy recognition and status; sit in the councils of administration; and make more than a modest contribution to industrial planning. Their age of growth and rebellion is over.

This assessment fits neatly into Galbraith's model by leaving out everything that does not fit. The broader needs of union members are not in harmony with the industrial system, or else *The New Industrial State* is a total waste of words. The unions remain a formidable instrument of reform. George Meany and his confidants may possess an enlightened outlook by nineteenth-century standards, but there is no guarantee that they will not be supplanted by more contemporary minds. This is a subject where prophecy is hazardous. It is true that the sectors of greatest union growth today are not within the industrial system as defined by Galbraith. But a method of classification cannot be a reason for ignoring significant facts. Moreover, suspicion is in order when claims are advanced concerning the essential nature of the proletariat, for it is not the first time that such claims have been made.

Having abandoned the unions to the establishment, Galbraith turns to the intellectuals. The educational and scientific estate is that part of the middle class connected with higher education and engaged in research and teaching. The number of teachers in higher education has grown from 24,000 in 1900 to an expected 920,000 in 1977, a fortyfold increase. Their constituency of students today is nine million. They are not only a sizable body but an influential one. Since the decisive factor of production in the mature corporation, as Galbraith sees it, is qualified talent, and since the educational and scientific estate supplies that talent, so it stands in similar relation

73

to the industrial system as did the bankers of old. Galbraith suggests that there is leverage in this position, but fortunately he qualifies it with the word potentially, for the educational and scientific estate cannot control the supply of talent as a banker controls the supply of savings. Yet the technostructure is dependent on educators for trained manpower and innovations, both social and technical, which arise in the university; hence, the potential influence of educators. The big question is how closely the educational and scientific estate will identify with the goals of the industrial system. The individualism valued by the educational elite may come into conflict with the technostructure's need for "organized public bamboozlement" which is distasteful to the intellectual community. While members of the technostructure are politically inhibited by their organizational ties to the corporation, members of the college and university community are not and their significant influence in opposing the Vietnam War proves that they are becoming a political force to be reckoned with.

Since Galbraith acknowledges that the educational and scientific estate lacks a sense of its own identity and is divided by various political views—part doing military research and another part opposing it—there is little to object to in his speculations. What is hard to credit is that any group in industrial society can be counted on for united action now or in the future. The educational and scientific estate is no more monolithic than the unions. Even part of the technostructure is restive as the siren song of consumer advocacy and professional accountability is wafted to its ears. It may be true that the main hope for scrutinizing the goals of the industrial system lies with the educational elite, but it is equally true that intellectual leadership in support of those goals also emanates from them. The search for a new vanguard is very tempting. I doubt if it will be found. Every class and stratum exhibits a distressing dualism. The future of the politics of change is not in the hands of a particular intrepid band which is somehow destined for historic leadership, but in a coalition which embraces all the progressives from street sweepers to investment bankers. Liberalism and conservatism simply do not follow class lines.

Galbraith's peroration is the expression of a hope for the future: a hope that the monopoly of the industrial system on social purpose will be broken; that the industrial system will be a diminishing part of life; that aesthetic goals will command increasing attention. "If other goals are strongly asserted, the industrial system will fall into its place as a detached and autonomous arm of the state, but responsive to the larger purposes of the society" (p. 402). In this view, the danger to liberty does not lie in the merger of big business and big government: that is a *fait accompli* and should be accepted as the inevitable outcome of technology and organization. The ultimate issue is how that technology and organization are to be used. "The danger to liberty"—and this is Galbraith's decisive point—"lies in the subordination of belief to the needs of the industrial system" (p. 401).

Behind all the technicalities of *The New Industrial State* there is a simple message: our success on the treadmill of production need not be the measure of life. We have the means to worthier ends if only we use them. Through education the industrial system has produced its own countervailing instrument capable of ending corporate domination.

CHAPTER 5

Conclusion

IN THE FIRST chapter we wrote that the economist who wants to discuss the economy in its institutional setting must tell a convincing story, weaving fact, value and theory into a coherent narrative which carries the reader along, inducing in him a warm glow of assent. Now we must ask to what extent this effect has been achieved by Galbraith. The reader who has persisted thus far is well aware that things went wrong as the story unfolded. It remains to try to find out why.

We characterized Galbraith as a revolutionary in economics because he is not simply dissatisfied with this or that aspect of theory, but with its very core.[1] His analyti-

---

1. To dispel any lingering doubts, Galbraith's own testimony may be in order: "I wish to argue that present professional belief—the neoclassical model of economic process—as profoundly accepted as was once the competitive model or Say's Law, is now similarly excluding urgent as well as politically disturbing questions from professional economic vision." *Economics, Peace and Laughter,* Houghton Mifflin, 1971, pp. 63-64. Needless to say, the quotation is not from the section on laughter.

cal starting point is the opposite from neoclassical theory. He begins with planning, not the market; the large firm, not the small; producer sovereignty, not consumer; the composition of output, not its magnitude. We need hardly add that Galbraith's intention is to start with assumptions derived from the real world of twentieth-century capitalism and to discard those which have their roots in the nineteenth century and require a mountain of qualifications to bring them up to date. In our opinion the task which Galbraith has set himself cannot be accomplished because the conception of the problem is wrong.

His cardinal error is to abandon the market as the organizing principle of the industrial system.[2] There is every justification in deriding the ancient claims for the market as a near-perfect regulator of price, quantity and assortment of output; but it is quite another matter to conclude that the market has lost its regulatory functions altogether and in fact has ceased to exist. The disappearance of the market is to be traced to Galbraith's conception of the mature corporation, really the cornerstone of his entire theoretical structure. The imperatives of technology and the uncertainties and frustrations of the market induce mature corporations to plan, and the plan replaces the market. They plan of course, but what they plan is not how to replace the market but how best to compete in it. And they do not always succeed, because the very technology which induces planning also fuels rivalry, and a preeminently successful giant like a railroad awakens one day and finds itself fighting for its life against the airplane.

2. A propensity to do so was displayed in the earlier concept of countervailing power.

If the mature corporation replaces the market with planning, then management's main concern no longer need be profit maximization. A new and different notion of corporate motivation and structure becomes possible. But if the corporation competes in a market, then the main tendency of behavior continues to be profit maximization, for it is nothing less than a necessity imposed by circumstances. That being the case, the right question is not what has replaced profit maximization as the main tendency of the corporation, but how is the tendency to profit maximization modified by oligopolistic conditions.

Another conclusion which flows from abolition of the market (we must always keep in mind that we are talking about the market with respect to the industrial system as defined by Galbraith, not the market and the entire economy) is the replacement of consumer sovereignty by producer sovereignty. Here Galbraith hedges. Pure Galbraithian theory would require a complete break with consumer sovereignty, but in the end he always draws back, and quite justifiably. Even though the producer influences the consumer, he does not have authoritarian control; the relationship is one of mutual influence. But Galbraith is entirely right in considering the old-fashioned picture of the hedonistic, rationalistic and atomistic consumer as nonsense. It is equally absurd to go to the other extreme and think of the consumer as a malleable blob subject to any extreme of outrageous manipulation. The butcher, the baker and the candlestick maker still think rationally about ends and means on occasion, and have individual personalities and preferences that still thwart the best efforts of Madison Avenue. The doctrine of consumer sovereignty, though battered, still contains a few nuggets of truth worth conserving.

The last bastion of standard economics to which Galbraith lays siege is macrotheory. His object is not to tear down the banner of fiscal policy but to place the banner of social balance beside it. Galbraith wants to go beyond Keynes. It is not enough to have full employment (or at least to try to have it). Social balance establishes new qualitative criteria to measure economic performance: minimum levels for the provisioning of goods and services; an aesthetically pleasing environment; the admission of interpersonal welfare comparisons.[3] The question may fairly be asked: are these issues of the same type as full employment? Though less susceptible to quantification, the answer must be yes. Full employment is not just an exercise in fiscal manipulation and statistics; it is also something thought to be good to have. It is just as much a matter of value as of theory. Here Galbraith blasts a swindle by showing that the hands-off attitude of conservative economics—which results in social *im*balance —rests on nothing more substantial than a set of alternative values masquerading as objective economic knowledge. When will economists and the public accept Galbraith's frame of reference? When the social tensions generated by failure to accept it become unbearable, just as Keynes' frame of reference became acceptable when tensions generated by the Great Depression rendered the previously held theory of unemployment obsolete. Thus Galbraith's main contribution to economics may well lie in a reconstruction of the underlying value sys-

---

3. Not to mention the fact that social balance also depends on ecological balance.

tem rather than in his work on the theoretical superstructure.

Galbraith is above all a publicist of post-Keynesian policies, and the merit of such policies does not depend on the elimination of the old economics root and branch. Keynes showed how aggregative planning can be used to achieve objectives of policy. Paradoxical as it may be, when we leave theory and get into policy, Galbraith talks like a man dealing with a market economy which he wishes to influence in certain ways by planning. Galbraith's anchor is Keynes, and Keynes stands for nothing if not managing market aggregates. The Galbraith formula $plan_1 + plan_2 \ldots + plan_n =$ planning has no operational significance when it comes to matters of policy. Policy flows from problems of a guided market economy, and Galbraith writes *as if* this were so, even though it is in flat contradiction to his more arcane pronouncements.

We may resolve the paradox by recognizing that there are really two Galbraiths (at least). One is the economist interminably embroiled in technical disputes with the economics profession; the other the advanced social critic lionized by the public for his witty sallies against humbug. Those who avoid confusing these two personae can recognize in the second Galbraith the possessor of a sweeping vision which perceives the outlines of a new model of production, a new model of consumption, a new ethical basis for economics and a broad prolegomenon of change.

We return to the point with which we began. Sometimes right, sometimes wrong, Galbraith has the courage to think big about the economy. It is futile to deny that separate problems must be studied separately. But the very nature of industrial society requires a coherent public policy, and that means, in the vernacular, putting it all together. Thinking big is inescapable in economics. And that is why the lower economics is here to stay.

Postscript

Economics and the Public Purpose

The Galbraithian Revolution

Bernard Shaw once wrote: "The reasonable man adapts himself to the world: the unreasonable one persists in trying to adapt the world to himself. Therefore all progress depends on the unreasonable man." Most economists will agree that John Kenneth Galbraith is an unreasonable man. They may, however, shrink from Shaw's conclusion that the unreasonable man is the cause of progress. In the present instance the issue will eventually be resolved by the place accorded *Economics and the Public Purpose*. It is the complete Galbraith. All his previous books are prelude. This one invites comparison with Keynes' *General Theory,* for it is Galbraith's general theory; and it is very general indeed. Previous economics is thrown unceremoniously on the rubbish pile. A new social order is sketched out in all necessary detail and the required methods of reform comprehensively presented. It has been a long time since so celebrated an

The author's review of Economics and the Public Purpose *originally appeared in* CHALLENGE: THE MAGAZINE OF ECONOMIC AFFAIRS, *September/October 1973.*

author has undertaken so much in a single book. If there is to be a Galbraithian revolution, it will be bigger than Keynes' by several orders of magnitude.

I hasten to add that there is nothing new or original in this book. It has all been said before in one way or another by James Madison, John Stuart Mill, Elizabeth Cady Stanton, Karl Marx, John Ruskin, Thorstein Veblen, Sidney and Beatrice Webb, Finley Peter Dunne, Joseph Schumpeter, Antonio Gramsci, C. Wright Mills, and countless others, any or all of whom Professor Galbraith may justly choose to disavow. No one carries all the genes of all his intellectual progenitors nor even knows who they all are. In fact I doubt that Galbraith came to his views through any particular intellectual tradition. Unlike many other critics of society's ills, he stands outside radical schools and movements. Ideologically he is a self-made man. He diagnosed the disease in his own way, mixed the medicine according to his own prescription, and offered it to the patient in his own good time. And that is about all the originality that any economist can hope for.

In the textbook world, the consumer and the citizen possess power; the corporation and the state do their bidding. In the Galbraithian world, the bureaucracies of the corporation and the state possess power; the consumer and the citizen are managed, manipulated, cajoled and persuaded. In the textbook world, the consumer maximizes his pleasures by choosing the shirts and soaps and soups and saloons that he likes best. In the Galbraithian world, the larger strategy of consumption is decided on high: the consumer will have cars and highways instead of trains and tracks because public and private authorities have invested the funds accordingly. In the textbook world, various branches of the economy develop in proportion to consumer need. In the Galbraithian world, they develop unevenly, in proportion to the power the producer commands. The consumer-citizen will enjoy the services of all the missiles he possibly can use because a strong munitions industry has a strong symbiotic relationship with a strong government bureaucracy—the Pentagon. He will go begging for housing because powerful housing corporations don't exist—nor do they have any powerful counterpart in the federal executive. All these contrasts can be easily summarized. In textbook economics, things have a tendency to work out for the best for everyone. But as Galbraith puts it, "Left to themselves, economic forces do not work out for the best except perhaps for the powerful."

"But," interjects an irate reader, "you have to be pretty stupid to take textbook economics at face value. Anyone in his right mind knows that all those propositions have to be qualified before they can be applied to reality." I'm sure Galbraith would agree. His point is that they have to be qualified so much that they are qualified out of existence. It is better to throw out the original assumptions and start with new ones that take the economy as it is.

If you wanted to compress Galbraith's message into three words, they would be power and uneven development. The economy is divided into two parts: the planning system and the market system. The first has about one thousand firms; the second twelve million. The thousand produce more of the gross national product than the twelve million combined. The four largest corporations in the planning system have total sales that exceed those of the three million farmers in the market system. These are the bare facts of power. Power resides in the planning system: the power to plan prices and outputs; to deploy modern technology and to grow; to sway consumers and the state. And the power to extract extremely favorable terms of trade from the market system. The two systems develop unevenly: the planning system from strength; the market system from weakness. The strong go to the state and get the services they need; the weak do without. Hence the highly uneven development of public services.

Galbraith, by the way, has at last integrated the housewife into modern economics. She is the administrator of consumption. Through a neat division of labor in the household, the husband seeks the ever-increasing utility of ever-increasing consumption because he does not suffer the ever-increasing disutility of managing more possessions. Housewives, converted into a crypto-servant class, become the unwitting allies of the planning system and its inexorable drive to proliferate the earth with more artifacts. When the odious connection between wifely virtue and corporate convenience dawns on American wives, the death knell of corporate power will have sounded.

The first two-thirds of *Economics and the Public Purpose* is devoted to how things are; the last third to how they ought to be. Much of the first two-thirds is plagiarized from *The New Industrial State*—Galbraith's own book, I hasten to add for the information of those who don't know—but Galbraith had to recapitulate so the stage could be set for his reforms. And the recapitulation smooths over many of the irritating spots of his last big book and offers enough qualifications of all propositions so that he can fall back to previously prepared positions, whatever and wherever the attack.

Most of the reforms can be classed as the five socialisms. But before coming to them, we must emphasize what Galbraith emphasizes: reforms depend on belief, not machinery. You can't get important reform by setting up a commission, putting a public representative on the board of directors, or making a list of regulations. "Law cannot anticipate understanding." The emancipation of belief comes first, which is to say that public opinion must change. Galbraith's quintessential conviction is that public opinion—belief—is now in the service of the planning system rather than in the service of the public itself. People are convinced that they need what the planning system can deliver—more commodities of the kind that the planning system is good at producing. This myth is perpetuated by economic pedagogy which teaches that the economy is best when intervention is least. But uneven development, inequality of income, the paucity of services, environmental disruption, inflation, the imbalance of payments and all the other economic horrors cause pain. "Pain," says Galbraith, "or even modest discomfort is better for persuasion than more abstract argument." The emancipation of belief is taking place because circumstance will have it so; Galbraith will just help it along.

The first job of those who attain public cognizance—Galbraithian shorthand for the state of mind of those who can distinguish the needs of the public from those of the planning system—is to pry the state loose from the grip of the planning system and place it at the disposal of the public. Emancipation of the state must be the central issue of the electoral process. Half a party already exists that is more or less ready to serve that purpose—the reform wing of the Democrats. More or less, because they grasp the situation only imperfectly—through political instinct—and need further exposure to the beneficial influence of rational economic thought. A sprinkling of Republicans are in the same class.

Now to the five socialisms. Galbraith's aims are to equalize power, competence and income; to safeguard the environment; to expand the use of public resources to serve public rather than private interests; and to stop the stop-and-go dilemma of inflation and deflation.

Socialism one—the new socialist imperative: run the weak parts of the market system by public authority, especially housing, urban transportation and medical care. Don't be pusillanimous about it. Face the fact that it must be done and do it well.

Socialism two—guild socialism: encourage small and weak firms to merge, form trade associations, fix output and prices, aid them with R&D and generally equalize their terms of trade with the planning system.

Socialism three—the elimination of bureaucratic symbiosis: nationalize the military contractors. They're public in everything but name anyway. The weapons bureaucrats work with Pentagon bureaucrats and together they hit Congress and the public from two sides for ever more money. One bureaucracy is better than two and will take off some of the pressure for support of a bloated military establishment.

Socialism four—the euthanasia of the stockholder: stockholders of large corporations have lost their social function. The rich who own most of the equity get richer on capital gains. Exchange their stock for fixed-interest-bearing public bonds and let the capital gains accrue to the public treasury. The corporations will go on being managed just as before, they will simply be public—like Renault in France or IRI in Italy—and more susceptible to the pressures of the public cognizance. Meanwhile the rich will dissipate their funds through estate taxes, divisions among heirs and high living, and we shall end up with greater equality of income and less concentration of illegitimate private power.

Socialism five—planning: the planning system needs to be planned. The automobile industry doesn't know what the petroleum industry is doing and the electric appliance industry doesn't know what the electric power industry is failing to do. Coordination is needed. Furthermore, wage and price increases can't be allowed to exceed average productivity increases, or we shall have a perpetual source of inflation. Wages and prices are privately administered in the planning system, and but a single step is required to administer them publicly in the public interest.

The five socialisms do not exhaust Galbraith's reforms. A minimum wage, a guaranteed income, abandonment of full employment, legal limits for the use and abuse of the environment, revenue-sharing, much less resort to monetary policy and others complete the battery of Galbraith's reforms.

Must I comment? Perhaps my job is done if I have managed to send you to *Economics and the Public Purpose* to read for yourself. This book will exert an enormous influence. There is planning in our future. Galbraith is quite blunt about it, much less urbane than usual. His work belongs to the genus mixed economy, in which, I need hardly add, planning bulks much larger than most American economists have dared contemplate. If there is a Galbraithian revolution, it will be bigger than Keynes' because Keynes let the market alone and was content to manage the level at which it operated. Galbraith would manage the market itself, and replace much of it with planning. Keynes also let most of the core of economic doctrine alone. Galbraith slashes away at its vitals—consumer sovereignty and the market—and damns it as flummery.

Those who shudder at the implications of such vast projects must remember that Galbraith is an optimist and a pragmatist. Never mind the dangers; we have to experiment. It is more dangerous to stand still. Never mind the risks of democratic public power; can't be worse than private. Never mind the dangers of centralized planning; if we abolish the extremes of wealth and poverty and have an aware public watching the planners, it will all come out right.

I leave the reader, Professor Galbraith and myself with Bertrand Russell's cautionary maxim: "It matters little what you believe, so long as you don't altogether believe it."

Conversation with an Inconvenient Economist

Q. *Economics and the Public Purpose* is a book of sweeping intent. It would consign existing economic theory and policy to the museum of antiquities and would replace them with new theory and new policy. These are revolutionary ambitions and yet you describe yourself as a reformer. How do you reconcile these two facts?

A. The main body of neoclassical or textbook doctrine is in the process of being replaced now; the sun is setting on that whole structure of thought. The notion that the individual is all-powerful, that the modern corporation is an automaton, subordinate to the market, can't survive. It is too drastically in conflict with common sense.

Once it is realized that economics as it is taught is part of the process by which people are persuaded to accept the structure of power in society—a vital part of the conditioning process which disguises that power—then the

The author's interview with John Kenneth Galbraith is reprinted from CHALLENGE: THE MAGAZINE OF ECONOMIC AFFAIRS, *September/October 1973.*

day of neoclassical economics is over. And that realization is coming—is certain. Already the phrase "neoclassical economics" is pejorative. A very large number of younger economists are in revolt. But I suppose the most compelling indictment is simply that neoclassical economics doesn't come to grips with the practical problems with which society, including the modern state, is faced. It doesn't come to grips with the unevenness in growth—as between, say, the housing industry and the automobile industry; it doesn't come to grips with the growing inequality in income distribution; it doesn't come to grips with the problems of coordination of different sectors of the economy now celebrated by such phrases as the energy crisis; it doesn't come to grips—except in a marginal way through the concept of external diseconomies—with the problems of environmental disharmony. It—notably—does not come to grips with the problem of controls—or even admit of their need. The major problem of modern economic policy is barely mentioned! We simply cannot have an economic theory that is nonfunctional.

It is not my instinct to be unduly modest, but let me say that I'm not authoring a revolution. Rather, I'm taking advantage of one that is already well along. Circumstances are the enemy of neoclassical economics, not Galbraith.

Q. You speak of the economy as being divided into two parts, a market system and a planning system. Would you explain why you make this division?

A. This is a vital conceptual technique. It is not meant

to imply that there is a sharp dividing line in the economy; but the distinction is indispensable. On the one hand we have agriculture, the service industries, artistically oriented industries, those industries that are not susceptible to large-scale organization. They conform roughly to the textbook image. And there is another world, that of General Motors and General Electric and General Dynamics and General Mills, something very different. One cannot deal with the modern economy until one accepts this dichotomy and examines the relations between its two parts.

Q. One of the central points that you stress is the uneven development of the market system and planning system. But aren't there many firms in the market system that do well, that use advanced technology, that have respectable profits?

A. As far as income is concerned, yes. There are returns to local monopoly, to what the classical economists called rare and exceptional talents, to extra diligence, to good fortune. High incomes, even spectacularly high incomes, can be obtained in the market system. Picasso was not a corporate executive, yet he had a remarkably high income. But, broadly speaking, there is less technology, a lesser technological dynamic in what I've called the market system. Agriculture is technologically progressive, but mostly because it gets technology from the big corporations—International Harvester, Deere—or because it uses socialized technology, technology developed by the state experiment stations or the United States government. Technological change is vastly greater in what I've called the planning system, in the roughly one thousand large corporations that contribute something over half of gross national product.

These corporations command resources. Resource use is not exclusively determined by consumer choice; it is influenced very strongly by producer power: by the power to persuade the consumer to buy; to persuade the state to lend support; to command earnings for reinvestment; to stabilize prices and costs and to plan resource use. It is this whole panoply of power that enables the enterprise to develop, and this development explains why we have an advanced automobile industry and the poor housing industry which I have mentioned. Houses aren't less wanted. That industry has much less power to command resources.

Q. The steel industry is not notable for its advanced technology. At the same time you can find many small firms in the market system which use high technology and in many cases were founded by engineers, chemists and physicists to apply techniques developed in universities.

A. I don't want to be rigid in these categories. There can be more and less technologically progressive firms in the planning system. I'm prepared to believe that the steel industry is one of the less progressive. Most of the technological dynamic of small firms, when one examines it, tends to come in one way or another from the planning system or the public sector. Either it is underwritten by large firms or, as you say, it is the overflow of work that has come out of the universities or it is sustained by (say) the Atomic Energy Commission or some other agency of the government.

Q. Referring to the market system again, you have quite a bit to say about the self-exploitation of the small businessman. Would you comment on that?
A. Yes. In this book I've examined the various factors which keep the small firm in being. One of these is that the small firm often operates outside the structure of rules that characterize organization. The organization has minimum or maximum requirements in wages, hours, and rate of work. It usually has a union, and a grievance procedure. One of the surviving advantages of the small firm is that it operates outside the rules emanating from the large corporation, the union or the government. The individual entrepreneur and his family can reduce their income, extend their hours of work, and otherwise exploit themselves as a means of survival.

Q. One more point about the market system. You put considerable emphasis on the arts as part of this realm.
A. There's an instinct that the last frontier of economic achievement has to do with science. There is, I think, a further frontier that is essentially artistic in character— the world of beauty and taste. The small entrepreneur, the individual, has very great advantages in this world. And many of the firms that survive in the market system have an artistic rather than a technological orientation. If I were a neoclassical economist defending my intellectual and commercial interest in what I know or what I had written in a textbook, I would place very much less emphasis on the inventive skills of the small entrepreneur and much more on his artistic advantages. This is the best prospect for the neoclassical entrepreneur. Agreeing that men of orthodox view must defend their

vested interest in existing knowledge, I don't think they do a particularly good job of it, and I'm going to help them out.

Q. You may just have extended the life of neoclassical economics by ten years. The planning system, if we may now turn our gaze in that direction, is made up of super-large firms in the heavily concentrated part of the economy. Why do you call it the planning system?

A. When I wrote *The New Industrial State,* I called it the industrial system. I suppose I didn't have the courage to give it the name that it should have. When one has control of prices or substantial authority over prices; control of costs or substantial influence over costs; when one goes beyond prices to influence the responses of consumers or the state; when one goes back beyond costs to organize supply, one no longer has market determination of resource use. The accepted name for that other kind of determination is planning. This is not the formal planning of the socialist state. It is a more informal and much less fully developed apparatus. But it is planning by organizations with the requisite power. One should call things by their right names.

The term also helps to focus on the planning problems that are developing in modern economic society. The expansion of the air-conditioning industry proceeds more rapidly than the expansion of the electric power industry; the expansion of the automobile industry proceeds more rapidly than the expansion of the oil industry. Therefore, we have problems of coordination among different planning sectors of the economy. Such problems don't arise in the market system; they are endemic to planning. So the use of the term "planning system" has the functional virtue of focusing attention on the kinds of problems that one would expect to emerge.

Q. This is precisely the point that gives me trouble. You have just said that there's an absence of planning in the planning system, there's a lack of coordination between the firms that produce air conditioning and those that produce electric power, or the ones that produce automobiles and those that provide fuel. Don't the large corporations in the part of the economy that you call the planning system still function in a market? They plan within the firm and they try to plan to function effectively in the market, but the relationships of the thousand or so firms in that system are unplanned and the relationships are still market relationships, are they not?

A. As we are talking here today, newspaper headlines carry the news of the appointment of a man variously described as an energy czar, or an energy coordinator. Governor Love would not be necessary in a market economy. The planning system that is emerging does not have a system of overall coordination; and that discrepancies in performance exist between different sectors—that the gears do not mesh—I concede, and indeed emphasize. But we must be precise in our terminology. One has a market system when the distribution of resources is impersonally governed by the decisions of individuals, of consumers. One has a planning system when the distribution of resources is increasingly controlled by the decisions of producers. That is the substantive difference; and although we have a planning system, we don't necessarily have a perfect one. The coordination is not perfect—it isn't perfect in the Soviet Union. Nor is the planning complete; market influences are not fully excluded. They are obviously still very important. But we must see the broad structural division between that part of the economy in which resource use is still subject overwhelmingly to market influences and that part which is becoming increasingly subject to the power of the productive apparatus, specifically the great corporation.

Q. Another major feature of the planning system is that the large corporation is controlled not by management, but by what you call a technostructure. Would you explain what the technostructure is, and how it controls the corporation?

A. This is not a terribly controversial point. As the corporation develops and matures, power passes from the stockholders to the management, and then it passes down into the bureaucratic apparatus of the corporation. This, in *The New Industrial State,* I termed the technostructure. The reason for this transmigration is that power is associated with knowledge. Knowledge grows out of the intellectual division of labor among those who guide the corporation. The stockholder, not being a participant in this process of organizing and sharing knowledge, becomes powerless. And so to a lesser extent does the senior brass. There are of course certain powers that top management retains—the power of casting personnel, initiating major change, reorganizing the bureaucracy. But the power of substantive decisions passes into the technostructure.

Q. It strikes me that you give us the technostructure with one hand but take it back with the other. Because if management in fact has the powers that you described, then it has plenary power to manage the corporation. It relies on technical personnel for information, and its decision-making is guided by that information. But if management in fact can do the things that you say it can do, then it really manages, doesn't it? And therefore power lies with management.

A. I'm tolerably experienced in the polemical aspect of economic discussion. If one doesn't use sharp categories, one is said to have left things unclear. And if one does use sharp categories, one is said to be simplistic. In fact, the locus of power in the corporation is not crystal clear, and not necessarily the same for different categories of decision. When technical matters are at issue, the power of technicians, engineers and scientists is great. If the problem is one of suborning the government, the power of the lawyers and lobbyists will be great. And of course the power of top management to change personnel remains. There is, in short, a diffusion of power within the technostructure which doesn't lend itself to any single very easy characterization. We do know that the tendency is for power to pass down into the technostructure.

Q. You argue that the purpose of the large corporation in the planning system is no longer to maximize profits as it was in a market system, but to pursue growth. But isn't the pursuit of growth indistinguishable from the long-run pursuit of profits?

A. No, I don't really think so. The accepted economics must defend profit maximization. If the firm maximizes profit, then it can be said to be wholly subordinate to the market. If other goals are possible, or if there's a choice of goals, then there's an independent exercise of power by the producing firm.

Growth, I may say, is the most plausible goal. A bureaucracy will seek to expand because this is the way it rewards itself. It rewards itself because growth means more pay, more promotions, more opportunity, more perquisites of office, more power—all of which are important. So growth satisfies the essential condition of self-interest for those who are in power. Profits, remember, go to the stockholder—the man who is losing power.

There are also two other important goals. First of all, there must be a relatively high threshold level of profits to keep the stockholders and creditors quiet, to avoid proxy fights, to avoid takeovers, to minimize recourse to banks, to secure the autonomy of the management and the technostructure. In addition, an increase in the profit level from year to year remains an important test of the efficacy of the management and the technostructure. It is therefore an important justification for their continued autonomy, power and independence. I'm also prepared to argue that technological virtuosity may on occasion be an end in itself. Corporations want to be known as smart outfits, as technologically progressive. However, I'm not disposed to rank that at the same level of importance as the other goals I've mentioned.

Now, a further point. It's a mistake to search for a unique solution to this problem. We are dealing with the order of a thousand corporations, some larger, some smaller, some more powerful, some less powerful, some more technically oriented than others, some extensions of the state, as in the case of General Dynamics or Lockheed. No one should conclude that the goal-structure of all these firms will be the same. Perhaps the market economy does yield a unique solution. It's an error—a very common one—to carry the search for a single solution into the world of the big corporation.

Q. You speak of the transnational system as an extension of the national planning system, and of the multinational corporation as the main element in this system. Will you elucidate?

A. The nature of the planning system, as I mentioned earlier, requires that it have control of as many things affecting it as possible: price, cost, supply, consumer response, and the multitude of needed services from the state. This is notably, perhaps even hilariously, inconsistent with the orthodox theory of international trade (the most depraved branch of neoclassical theory), which assumes, by and large, that products are carried to the shore, put on a boat, and sold in second countries for what the market will yield. It's idle to suppose that there would be a high degree of certainty in national trade and a high degree of uncertainty in international trade. In fact, firms follow their products into the second countries, re-create the firm there where it becomes part of the oligopoly equilibrium. And it is able to persuade consumers, and bring influence to bear, as required, on the community and the state. Thus the multinational corporation is the plausible extension of the national corporation; it wins the same kind of security in its transnational environment as it does at home. In addition, it can meet competition by going where the cost of labor is lowest and the conditions of production are most efficient. This elides two of the problems of classical international trade. To summarize: the multinational corporation is simply the means by which the modern corporation minimizes the uncertainties peculiar to international trade.

Q. You've now described the two parts of the economy: the market system and the planning system. What is the relation between them?

A. There is endemic inequality between the two systems in power and thus in economic development, technical dynamic, income, and security of income. The terms of trade greatly favor the planning system, which, among other things, has the capacity to take advantage of what I've called the self-exploitative tendencies of the market system. There are also vital differences in the relations to the state. The bureaucracies of the planning system work closely with public bureaucracies, with attendant advantages. Firms in the market system do not have such access—to the Pentagon, for example. They must deal with the legislature, a much more cumbersome way of doing business.

Q. I would say that the central theme of your book is uneven development between the two systems: unequal power, unequal income, unequal opportunity in almost every respect. The conclusion is that left to itself, the market doesn't work to the benefit of anybody except the powerful. How does this theory of uneven development compare with the theory of social imbalance which you advanced in *The Affluent Society*?

A. A very good question. The theory of social imbalance advanced in *The Affluent Society* was a first cut at the problem. Fortunately, no arrangement has yet been worked out to require authors to withdraw books to correct defects. Automobile companies, yes; but not economists. In *The Affluent Society* I saw an imbalance between the services of the state and the production of commodities and services in the private sector. This notion is still valid. But I did not then see that there are some services of the state—those that are subject to the power and serve the need of the planning system—which do not suffer from this underdevelopment. Where service is rendered to the planning system, as in the case of highways, or where products of the planning system are purchased, as in the case of weapons, public functions are very powerfully developed. Where the state serves the market system or the public at large—where it relates to weakness—its services are much less fully developed. What I offer here is a more complex view of the theory of social balance. It is now right and not subject to further revision!

Q. One of the most novel and intriguing parts of *Economics and the Public Purpose* is your treatment of the household, and your reintegration of the household into economic theory. You speak of housewives as a crypto-servant class and you coin a new Galbraithian phrase, "the convenient social virtue."

A. These are very important matters and point up one of the minor crimes of the accepted economics. Nothing is so featured as the ultimate authority of the individual in society, the ultimate authority of the individual in markets, the ultimate authority of the individual in the political process. Then, after all power has been so admirably reposed in the individual, comes a deft sleight-of-hand: the individual is made coordinate with the household; it is assumed that the preference schedules of a man and wife, indeed, of all members of the household, are the same. And this in turn becomes a fascinating and subtle disguise for the role of women in economic life.

As the standard of living rises and the volume of consumer goods increases, so do the problems in administering consumption. The management of the automobile, the extirpation of the crabgrass, the upkeep of the house, the repair of household furnishings, the cleaning of clothes, the preparation of food, and the competitive display of social talent that is an aspect of refined living—all tend to fall as burdens on the woman—or anyhow, the larger share. So it comes to pass that the person we call the head of the household—the man—enjoys the consumption, and the work associated with consumption falls on the woman. And this makes possible a very much greater increase in consumption (and production) than would be possible were the full burden of administration to fall on the person who enjoys the consumption. All this is concealed by the device, really very engaging, of making the household coordinate with the individual. The marriage bed unites men and women and their preference schedules and their personalities; and one never need look further.

Were it recognized in economic pedagogy that increasing consumption is possible only because of the increasing role of women as administrators of consumption, and were this taught to the several hundred thousand women who study economics each year, there might be a general rejection by women of this role. But, by incorporating women into the household, and then making the household synonymous with the individual, the whole problem is very neatly finessed. One is almost unhappy about letting the light shine in on it.

Q. Where does the "convenient social virtue" come in?
A. The convenient social virtue is a very useful idea. Any group with power in the society tends to make virtuous what it finds convenient. It was virtuous behavior in the last century to be very frugal. This was the convenience of those who needed capital accumulation—for saving. It has become virtuous in this century for people to spend freely, to have a good American standard of living. This is the virtue that is convenient to the modern large producer of consumer goods. The convenient social virtue of modern woman is to be a good homemaker or a good manager or a good organizer, or a good wife, which is to say she capably administers the high level of consumption that modern economic society requires. When one gets hold of the relation between economic convenience and virtue it's surprising how often they coincide.

Q. Now we come to the subject that this entire discussion has been leading up to, what you describe as the general theory of reform. You argue that before any particular mechanism of reform can work, it has to be preceded by what you call the emancipation of belief. You stress that today belief—commonly accepted social and economic opinion—is in the service of the planning system. Before any basic reforms can take place, belief has to be freed from its subservience to the goals of the planning system. You call this the public cognizance. Would you explain why this is central to your doctrine of reform?

A. It is central because the major instrument for the exercise of power by the planning system is persuasion. One of its simplest forms is advertising. But there are many other forms, including the subtle but very important tendency for what is considered sound public policy to be that policy which best serves the purposes of the great firms in the planning system. One extremely important manifestation of this persuasion is the accepted economics. Its conclusions—the subordination of the firm to the market, for example—are those which disguise the power exercised by the planning system. And power that is disguised is power that is exercised with greater freedom and greater safety than power that is identified. To identify power is to invite people to react against it.

The whole process of persuasion is instrumental to the exercise of power, and it's obvious that nothing much is going to be changed until that fact is recognized. The clearest case of this concerns the state. As I said a moment ago, sound public policy tends to be that policy which best serves the planning system. The purposes of the planning system, in turn, are frequently in conflict with those of the public. A recognition of this fact is absolutely essential to the recapture of the state for public purposes. This is necessary because the state remains the essential instrument of reform.

I refer to the perception of the difference between the public purpose and the corporate purpose as the public cognizance. The public cognizance, in turn, is decisive for political understanding and effective public action.

Q. When you use the phrase "the public cognizance," who is the public? Are there particular groups, classes, or strata of the public that are likely to recognize that the emancipation of belief is necessary in order for the public to serve its self-interest?

A. Oh yes. There are in any society groups that exercise leadership, and groups that tend to be acquiescent in the leadership of others. One such leadership group would be the academic, scientific, journalistic, and professional community where ideas of this sort first take hold. People who do not want change, who want to perpetuate the existing myth, always say: "Don't pay any attention to the nonsense of the so-called thinkers. They're always wrong." People who want to stand pat are, as Keynes said, the slaves of the defunct thinkers or those who serve their interest. In fact, most ideas do begin with a relatively small group and spread out from there.

Q. You refer to the Republican Party as an instrument of the planning system, and part of the Democratic Party as an instrument of the planning system. That leaves half a party, the reform wing of the Democratic Party, as the political group which potentially will accept the public cognizance. Do you think this is sufficient to bring about the kinds of reforms that you propose? Would you like to see other groups—say an American Fabian Society—advocate the program you have outlined?

A. The Republican Party rather openly identifies the purposes of the planning system with the public interest. So does a considerable part of the Democratic Party without quite realizing it. On the other hand, there is a growing group within the Democratic Party, and perhaps also in the liberal wing of the Republican Party, that does recognize—if not explicitly, then as a matter of political instinct—that there is a conflict between the public purpose and that of the great corporation. And this perception has been growing. It's my hope, indeed my expectation, that the perception of this conflict will become increasingly clear and that the division in our politics will be increasingly between those who insist on the purposes of the planning system and those who identify themselves with the public purpose.

Whether new political organizations will come into being to advance this change I couldn't possibly say. I'd be for something more dynamic than the Fabians now are.

Q. You have a rather comprehensive strategy for reforming the market and planning systems. What major reorganization would you like to see take place within the market system?

A. The great strengthening of the bargaining position of the market system vis-à-vis the planning system. This entails measures which arrest the tendency to self-exploitation. The guaranteed minimum income is important here as an alternative to unacceptably low income associated with self-exploitation and the bargaining weakness of the market system in general.

To equalize growth and development between the two systems is a matter of central importance. This has caused me to argue for what I've called the new socialist imperative. This does not seek out the parts of the economy where there is power, which has always been the instinct of the person who is oriented to strong social action. Rather, it seeks out the weak parts and brings the resources of the state to support development. Circumstances have, as usual, already forced the pace. When one looks at the areas of public social action, one doesn't find the government trying to make General Motors more efficient, or General Electric or General Mills. The main area of government activity is in the fields of housing, agriculture, health and the like. We are already putting most of our social energies into shoring up the weak sectors of the economy. Practical reform has anticipated the theoretical argument—as it often does.

Q. One of the proposals that you offer is that small and weak firms in the market system be encouraged to combine, that the antitrust laws be set aside in these cases, that they form trade associations, that they be encouraged to fix prices and output. Doesn't this have the danger of creating rigidities which would have a negative effect on resource allocation? In another instance you deplore the fact that the American Medical Association acts as a guild to restrict necessary developments. Isn't there the risk that similar guilds in other cases would be self-serving?

A. You may have somewhat overstated the case that I make. I would not abandon supervision in this area. But as long as we accord ITT the power that it has under the antitrust laws, it's surely wrong to deny small firms dealing with ITT the right to combine to seek improvement in their terms of trade or to try to limit self-exploitation as a form of competition.

Q. The total of reforms that you suggest for the market system, which include such things as mergers, trade associations, a minimum wage, and increased unionization, would result in higher prices in the market system. One result of this would be unemployment in those fields where people are simply unwilling to pay the prices required for particular goods or services. To remedy this, you propose a guaranteed income as an alternative for those who cannot find employment. As a matter of fact you refer to the market system as the employer of last resort. You consign to a footnote the use of public service employment. Do I understand correctly that you're giving precedence to guaranteed income over public service employment?

A. No. I would regard that as a most important footnote.

Q. What kinds of action would you say are necessary to reform the planning system?

A. Since the market system is the weakest part of the economy, the one which is subject to discrimination as regards both development and income, this not surprisingly is the major focus of reform. But the other side of the coin is excessive social support for the planning system. This is the result of the particular power that is exercised over the state; it means that public resources which support the planning system must be reallocated systematically to the support of the market system. Highways for the auto industry are a case in point. The weapons industry is another. Space exploration is another case. Outlays for research and development now strongly orient toward the planning system. It's a commonplace that when large firms in the planning system—Lockheed, for example—get into trouble, they turn to the state for support. These are all instances of excessive allocation of public resources to the planning system—all reflections of its ability to make its needs become sound policy.

I also argue that we would reduce and make much more visible the power of some parts of the planning system by taking firms into full public ownership. A particular case here is the big weapons firms. Working capital is supplied by the government; a large fraction of their fixed capital is supplied by the government; their business comes from the government. Yet the fiction is maintained that they are private firms. This fiction allows them to lobby, encourage lobbying by unions, promote political contributions and candidates and otherwise engage in activities that would be forbidden to full public firms. I see public ownership as a device for reducing the power presently deployed by one part of the planning system.

Beyond this, I suppose the day will come when the really mature corporation will be recognized for what it is—a public corporation. We should not imagine that General Motors in its present form is the final word of God and man, although that is a fine example of the reputable view.

Q. One element in your proposed reform of the planning system is to bring about the euthanasia of the stockholders of mature corporations. You would have the government buy the stock with fixed-interest-bearing bonds. Stockholders would then be denied capital gains, and a major source of income inequality would be eliminated. But the stockholders have no role in your analysis of the modern economy. Why not bring up the low incomes and let the rich alone?

A. The idea here—it's a suggestion really—is essentially simple. In the fully mature corporation the stockholder performs no function. The holding of stock becomes a device by which the investor gets his revenue in the form of capital gains, as you said, and therefore gets preferential treatment in his income tax. It would be an honest and straightforward remedy to convert private stockholders into public bondholders and have the capital gains accrue to the state. And the experience in any number of state-owned corporations—Volkswagen in the past, Renault, British Petroleum in large part—indicates that firms that are state owned function with no perceptible difference from firms that are owned by functionless stockholders. As to your final suggestion that the rich should be left alone and the poor be brought up—this is the old liberal formula, and it simply isn't working.

Q. Would you accept it if it worked?
A. No. On the whole I'm committed to the idea of a much greater equality of income as an independent social good. Also, I'm forced to this position by the general logic of the analysis, for it associates income with power. The obvious example is in the corporation itself, in which income is associated with the power of the individual in the corporate bureaucracy. But the distribution of income between the market system and the planning system is also associated with power. So if one is seeking to equalize power and the exercise of power, one is seeking *pro tanto* to equalize income.

Q. There are several kinds of socialism that you propose in *Economics and the Public Purpose.* One is what you call the new socialism, which would put those parts of the market system that function inadequately, such as housing, local transportation, and medical facilities, under public administration. Another is what you call guild socialism, in which you would encourage small firms in the market system to work together, to cooperate. A third is in the case that you describe as bureaucratic symbiosis, where the bureaucracy of the large firm—in particular the military contractor—works hand in hand with a government bureaucracy, such as the Pentagon. In the final case you would convert large mature corporations into public firms by buying out the stockholders. Doesn't this involve a great deal of centralization and bureaucracy and all the dangers that go with centralization and bureaucracy?

A. No. I would say this just makes visible what now exists. The mature corporation does not become more bureaucratic by having its stock publicly owned. And the present organization for providing medical services, housing services, public transportation and the like involves an intricate combination of public and private organizations. In housing, to use one example, it would be simpler to follow the European model and recognize that construction and maintenance of medium- and lower-cost housing must be a straightforward public operation. Put public corporations in charge. See that they do it well.

As far as allowing smaller firms to combine to regulate prices, good lord, the large corporations already have this power. This doesn't add to bureaucracy; it simply permits the small man to enter into the same defensive arrangements that the large corporation takes for granted. However, if there is a choice between less centralized private power and more centralized public power—power that responds to the public cognizance and interest—one should choose the latter. But I don't think this is really the issue.

Q. You choose to use the pejorative term socialism to describe a number of the things you would like to do. Wouldn't it have been more tactful to use a euphemism? *A.* Oh, I suppose so. This is something to which I gave more than passing thought. But even in terminology one should try to reflect the reality, to use the plain language that does so. If this is socialism, let it be called that. We're discussing economics, not a party platform.

√√
reform

Q. One startling proposal in your list of reforms is that you want to give up the goal of full employment. Why do you think this is necessary? Wouldn't it be possible to retain the goal of full employment by using the government as employer of last resort?
A. I would make use of public service employment. Still, there is a conflict between the goal of full employment and the unsatisfactory terms on which employment takes place in the weak or self-exploitative parts of the market. I would have some unemployment as the price of maintaining the standards of those who are employed. Unemployment with an adequate guaranteed income may be more civilized than employment with an inadequate one.

I remember a year or two ago, at the meetings of the American Economic Association in New Orleans, I was having my shoes shined by an elderly arthritic man at the shoeshine stand across from the hotel. Had he any alternative income, this poor old man would be unemployed. Is this such a bad thing? Instead of having to accept a derogatory form of employment, he would have an alternative. Such unemployment seems to me desirable. It confines the employment of people as shoeshine operators to the number who can be paid a decent wage.

Q. The capstone of your program of reforms is centralized planning of the planning system. Could you explain how this is to be done?

A. This brings us to the frontiers of present policy. Because it is a planning system, there is no assured mechanism (as in the market system) for coordination among its different parts. So the automobile industry produces very large automobiles in very large numbers with very large gasoline consumption, in response to its particular planning dynamic. And the petroleum industry produces gasoline subject to environmental constraints, diminishing reserves, international complications, in short, in accordance with a different dynamic. There is nothing in this mechanism—since price does not operate to bring an adjustment—to ensure that the supply of gasoline will any longer equal the needs of the automobile industry. And so while solemn scholars will be resisting the thought of a planning system in the United States, of all places, an energy czar appointed by Mr. Nixon (not, presumably, the world's foremost advocate of planning even after his education by Mr. Brezhnev) will be trying to bring about the coordination of gasoline requirements and supply. There is a similar discrepancy between the dynamic of the electric power industry and that of the electric appliance industry, including the needs of air conditioning. Soon we will have coordinators here. There is a similar prospect in transportation. Maybe in lumber and paper. Out of all this will one day emerge some overall body for anticipating these disparities among different industries, anticipating them and forestalling them. Then maybe we'll even get around to using the word "planning." Circumstance is making all this quite commonplace. The surprise lies only in its being so inconsistent with conventional economic pedagogy. Shouldn't economics anticipate problems of this sort, or at least be abreast of them?

Q. Any reader who has followed us this far will realize that you have proposed both sweeping reforms in economic theory and sweeping reforms in the social order. How do you assess the prospects of success?

A. Let's take the second first. Reform is inevitable, because the problems are real. When automobiles start running out of gasoline or housing is ghastly or medical services unaffordable or the rich become too obscenely rich in relation to the rest, something gets done about it. Social pressures build up, politicians respond, so the kinds of actions which are required get taken. The action may be disguised by the semantics. It will be some time before we get around to talking about planning. It will be longer, no doubt, before we get around to using so obscene a word as socialism. I sometimes use the phrase "social action," which is more benign. Even talk about income redistribution seems to many people still very odd and dangerous. But circumstances are in the saddle, not theory.

As to the change in economics, there is a new generation of economists for whom the term "neoclassical economics" has already become pejorative. It is increasingly difficult to persuade students into belief. Even at Harvard our graduate students are showing an appalling tendency to question the worth of the neoclassical models. Once we spoke of economics as something that described reality. Now we refer to neoclassical economics (or orthodox or accepted economics) as something which serves the purposes of the textbooks, which occupies students and professors but which is not imagined greatly to illuminate life as it is. So there is an indication of change even here. But we must recognize how change occurs in economics. Scholars do not often change their minds. Men remain with their obsolescence—alas. Change comes from the changing of generations. Very few people of Keynes' generation accepted Keynes—if I may be allowed a pretentious reference. It was the next generation that came along and thought his ideas were interesting. I have very little hope of persuading the people of my generation that power and the many things flowing from it must be brought within the framework of economics along the lines that we've been discussing. But that is not important. People of the next generation have already shown that they are open to a new, or anyhow a revised, view of economic life. They will be persuaded; power will become, in one way or another, part of their system, for power exists. I have every hope— indeed, I have every expectation—of persuading those who are younger. With the passage of time, there will be a new orthodoxy—a chilling thought.

Index

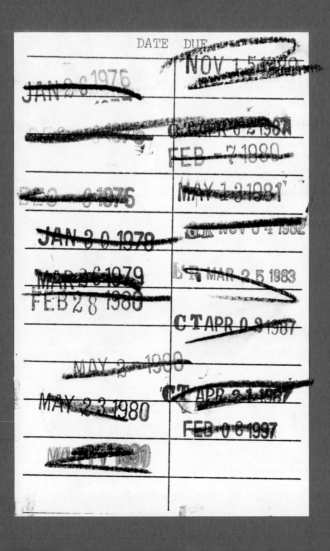